Why Does Tragedy Give Pleasure

Why Does Tragedy Give Pleasure?

A. D. NUTTALL

CLARENDON PRESS · OXFORD

This book has been printed digitally and produced in a standard specification in order to ensure its continuing availability

OXFORD
UNIVERSITY PRESS

Great Clarendon Street, Oxford OX2 6DP

Oxford University Press is a department of the University of Oxford.
It furthers the University's objective of excellence in research, scholarship,
and education by publishing worldwide in

Oxford New York

Auckland Bangkok Buenos Aires Cape Town Chennai
Dar es Salaam Delhi Hong Kong Istanbul Karachi Kolkata
Kuala Lumpur Madrid Melbourne Mexico City Mumbai Nairobi
São Paulo Shanghai Taipei Tokyo Toronto

Oxford is a registered trade mark of Oxford University Press
in the UK and in certain other countries

Published in the United States
by Oxford University Press Inc., New York

© A. D. Nuttall 1996

The moral rights of the author have been asserted
Database right Oxford University Press (maker)

Reprinted 2003

ISBN 0-19-818766-1

Et dolet et specto; iuvat et spectasse dolendo
Milton, *Elegia Prima*

PREFACE

This short book was once, so to speak, even shorter. It began when I received a letter from Karl Miller inviting me to give the Northcliffe Lectures for 1992 in University College, London. Those three lectures have now grown into four chapters. My disagreement with Martha Nussbaum over the meaning of the word *catharsis* in Aristotle, offered far too lightly in the lecture hall, is now argued in detail. Nussbaum's book, *The Fragility of Goodness*, is itself written with so much force and fairness of mind that any dissent is obliged to present itself with care. The section on Freud is now more carefully shaded, more guarded than the original few paragraphs. Despite these protestations, some readers will inevitably say that really a great deal *more* care, *more* detail is required for so large a subject. It will be obvious that I have chosen to retain the general form of a brief lecture series, to write an essay in which, unsubduably, the voice of a live speaker is still occasionally audible, rather than to attempt an exhaustive treatise.

Stephen Halliwell, whose views were misrepresented in the first edition of the book, generously drew my attention to various mistakes. One reader of my manuscript felt that I ought to say more about French tragedy; I thought myself that I ought to be saying more about Hume. I could have remedied both these defects but the result, I believe, would have to be a retardation and blurring of what is still, as things stand, a unified argument.

I have been helped by people in lecture halls whose names I do not know, by friends, by the admirable, anonymous persons who read manuscripts for the Oxford University

Press, by William Race of Vanderbilt University, and above all by Anthony Storr, who responded swiftly to all my queries with both sharpness and humanity. The surviving errors are of course mine, not his.

The third chapter, 'The Game of Death', appeared (without its apparatus of notes and references) in *The London Review of Books*, 11 June 1992.

A.D.N.
New College, Oxford

CONTENTS

1
ARISTOTLE AND AFTER

If we were all wicked, there would perhaps be no problem. A world of torturers would naturally be pleased by the blinding of Oedipus or else, to take a cooler form of wickedness, it would not be surprising if an audience inwardly driven by envy were to delight in the fall of one greater than they. But why does tragedy give pleasure to 'people like ourselves'?

A cruel or sadistic pleasure in the blinding of Oedipus is immediately distinguishable from what Aristotle called the *oikeia hedone*, 'the proper pleasure' of tragedy (*Poetics*, 1459 a 21) and I fancy that the same is true—though less obviously true—in the case of the gloating, envious spectator. In the tragic theatre suffering and death are perceived as matter for grief and fear, after which it seems that grief and fear become in their turn matter for enjoyment.

'The pleasure of tragedy' is an immediately uncomfortable phrase. Quite apart from the original basic collision between terrible matter and a delighted response, there is an awkwardness, somehow, in the very mildness of the term 'pleasure'—it seems a puny word to set beside the thunderous term 'tragedy', adding a species of insult to injury. The Nietzschean oxymoron, 'tragic joy' is, oddly, easier to accept, because it fights fire with fire. I suspect moreover that the awkwardness has become more obvious in our century. For moral Dr Johnson it was self-evident that poetry and drama must please. A later kind of moralism taught a new generation of readers and theatre-goers to despise the pleasurable and to value the disturbing, the jagged, the painful work. It is now virtually unimaginable that a reviewer of a new play should praise it by saying that it offers solace or comfort. Conversely the adjective 'uncomfortable' is automatically read as praise. Ancient Stoics and Epicureans argued about most things but they would be united in their bewilderment at this. I am a twentieth-century person and I share the general taste for discomfort. But the radical problem remains obstinately in place: if people go again and again to see such things, they must in some way enjoy them. Similarly, if you like the disturbing kind of play then *this* disturbance is something you like, must itself be a further mode of pleasure. The shift in taste does not resolve the problem of tragic pleasure; rather it sets an allied, similarly challenging problem—that of enjoyed discomfort—alongside it.

Many things, when looked at hard, seem to come to bits (or, as we now say, 'to undergo deconstruction'). Certainly this is true of the notion of pleasure. 'Quantity of pleasure being equal, push-pin is as good as poetry,' said Jeremy Bentham,[1] robustly. Here pleasure is offered for inspection as a luminously simple datum: of course poetry and push-pin are profoundly different things, but, meanwhile, pleasure is pleasure, *semper idem*. But the datum can prove strangely elusive. For example, while it may seem essential to the idea of pleasure that it be felt, pleasure need not occupy the foreground of *consciousness*, which will afford simultaneous space for objects of another kind. I mean by this only that one can enjoy an activity or process without at any point thinking consciously, 'I am enjoying this', or 'this is very agreeable'; instead one may be thinking only of the activity itself. When two people converse we may observe that they enjoyed the conversation intensely, but if *per impossibile* one obtained entry to their fields of consciousness one would never find at any point a separately introspected element, 'the pleasant', but instead an unbroken

[1] Quoted by John Stuart Mill in his essay, 'Bentham', in the *Westminster Review*, 1838.

preoccupation with the subject of the conversation itself. As Gilbert Ryle wrote, 'When I enjoy or dislike a conversation, there is not, beside the easily clockable stretches of the conversation, something else, stretches of which might be separately clocked, some continuous or intermittent intro-spectible phenomenon which is the agreeableness or disagreeableness of the conversation to me.'[2] Ryle was notoriously hostile to the very idea of an interior field of consciousness and may therefore have put the case in too absolute a form. David Hume once made a special expedition, as it were, into his introspective world to see if at any point he could discover anything—any thing—he could call a 'self', with 'Rylean' negative results.[3] Hume however was willing to allow (in an earlier part of the *Treatise*) a more diffuse consciousness: 'In thinking of our past thoughts we not only delineate out the objects, of which we were thinking, but also conceive the action of the mind in the meditation, that certain *je-ne-scais-quoi*, of which 'tis impossible to give my definition or description, but which everyone sufficiently understands.'[4] Whether we go for a Rylean exclusion of pleasure-consciousness or a quasi-Humean relegation of such consciousness to the fringes of awareness, it is clear that intense enjoyment is compatible with a mind dominated by objects in themselves neutral. Some objects—sex-objects, say, or food-objects—are so regularly linked with pleasure as to cause the distinction I have offered to disappear; we would find it easy and natural to say that the small boy eating Christmas pudding is immediately conscious of pleasure even if his inner preoccupation is as adequately represented by the word 'pudding' as it is by the word 'pleasure'. Enjoying a game of chess, on the other hand, seems not to yield the same, almost automatically

[2] *Dilemmas: The Turner Lectures* (Cambridge: Cambridge University Press, 1960), p. 59.

[3] *A Treatise of Human Nature*, I. iv. 6, ed. L. G. Selby-Bigge (Oxford: Clarendon Press, 1888), p. 252.

[4] Ibid., I. iii. 10, p. 106.

fused, result. 'White Queen to Queen's Bishop's 4th' is not immediately charged with the pleasure message in the way Kevin Costner, say, is for some people or Newcastle Brown Ale for others.

If, then, more neutral objects—that is to say, objects which are not seen as themselves constituting 'pleasures'—may be admitted to a dominant place in the subject's consciousness without any necessary diminution of that subject's actual pleasure, it becomes a little easier, perhaps, to think that pleasure may lie as much in some concomitant action or process as it does in the brightly illuminated area of consciousness.

It rather looks as if Aristotle's explanation of our enjoyment of tragic suffering and death is an answer of this kind. In that extraordinary surviving 'sheaf of lecture notes or lecture handouts dating from the 4th century BC called the *Poetics*, we find one of the first theories of social psychology. The Greek is crabbed and elliptical; one can sometimes hear the testy accent of the crotchety teacher—*hoper eiretai pollakis* (1456 a 10–11), 'as I have told you many times'. We also become aware as we read of a double rhetoric. Aristotle is teaching the young and, simultaneously, he is arguing with his own dead teacher, Plato. I have some sympathy with him: I spent the first ten years or so of my adult life arguing in my head with the man who taught me Latin and Greek at school. The story of the difference between Plato and Aristotle over poetry is a familiar one, so I will try to make it short. Plato, whom we know to have been a superb poet, feared poetry and would not permit it in his ideal commonwealth. It is important to remember that the banishing of the poet is described by Plato not coolly but with evident grief.

If one should come to our city [he wrote] who has power to become anyone, to represent all things, wishing to show himself and his poems to us, we will kneel to him as to a sweet, holy and wonderful being and will tell him that he and his kind have no place, according to our law, in our city. And so, having anointed him with myrrh and crowned him with flowers, we shall send him away to another city.

(*Republic*, 398A)

Plato feared poets because it seemed to him that they told lies and whipped up irrational emotions.

Aristotle's answer is that, in tragic poetry at least, emotion is not whipped up, but is *discharged*. His word, which has become so famous that it has stepped from Greek into English, is *catharsis*, 'purification' or 'purgation'. The word occurs in his famous, endlessly contraverted definition of tragedy at *Poetics*, 1449 b 24–8. Translating as literally as possible, we get: 'Tragedy, then, is an imitation of an action which is serious and (as having magnitude) complete, in sweetened language, each kind of sweetening being introduced separately in the parts of the work, of persons performing actions and not through report, through pity and fear accomplishing the *catharsis* of such emotions' (*pathemata* in the Greek). Where I have said, 'of persons performing actions and not through report', Bywater says 'in a dramatic, not in a narrative form'. Bywater's version misses, I think, the 'first-time', 'hewn from the rock' feeling of the Greek. The Greek word *drama*, having the sense 'theatrical performance', is found before Aristotle, but this use seems to be rare. The primative sense, 'doing', must still have been prominent. Of the two translations of *catharsis* I gave, 'purgation' is the more likely to be correct. Certain highminded commentators—notably Heinsius, Victorinus, Lessing, Batteux, Susemihl, and, in the present century, Humphry House—have been anxious to show that Aristotle had in mind a purification or sanctification of the emotions.[5]

---

[5] For the 'medical' interpretation, see Jacob Bernays, *Zwei Abhandlungen über die aristotelische Theorie des Drama* (Berlin: W. Herz, 1880), esp. pp. 11–13. See also Ingram Bywater's note to *Poetics*, 1449 b 27, in his translation with commentary *Aristotle on the Art of Poetry* (Oxford: Clarendon Press, 1909) and the same author's 'Milton and the Aristotelian Definition of

But it is clear enough, from a heavily medical use of the same word in another work of Aristotle, the *Politics* (1342 a, cf. 1341 a 24, 1341 b 32) that the philosopher's thoughts lie more in the direction of castor oil than of holy water. The medical interpretation, championed by Tyrwhitt, Bernays, and Weil, was known in the sixteenth century—to Minturno, for example.[6] For Aristotle it is not the emotions which are purified but the organism. The emotions themselves are, precisely, the impurity which is removed. That emotions are unpleasant for Aristotle seems to me a direct and inescapable implication of the medical term here used. He is thinking like a civic governor and is saying to his dead teacher, Plato, 'You've got the psychology wrong; people leaving a tragic performance don't smash shops and beat up peaceable passers by; they are strangely quiet.' 'Calm of mind all passion spent',[7] was Milton's version at the end of *Samson Agonistes*, where the word 'spent' may alert us to the faint possibility of an analogy not just with excretion but with sexual discharge. Since the Oxford English Dictionary does not support the sense 'sexually ejaculate' for the verb *spend* and does not allow it for the substantival form of the word before 1879–80, I will give my evidence for believing that nevertheless this sense was available and could therefore have operated not, I would guess, as a deliberately planted ambiguity, but rather as a half-articulated thought at the back of Milton's mind. The sexual meaning seems to me to be clearly present in Parolles' words in *All's Well that Ends Well*, II. iii. 279, 'spending his manly marrow in her arms'. Parolles is here urging Bertram to scorn amorous

---

Tragedy', *Journal of Philosophy*, vol. xxviii (1909), pp. 267–78. See also Stephen Halliwell, *Aristotle's Poetics* (London: Gerald Duckworth, 1986), Appendix 5, pp. 350–6, and Humphry House, *Aristotle's Poetics* (London: Rupert Hart-Davis, 1964), esp. p. 110.

[6] *A. Sebastiani Minturni de Poeta Libri Sex* (Venice, 1559). Minturno uses the word *purget*, 'purges', on p. 63 and pursues the medical analogy in detail on the following page.

[7] The last line of *Samson Agonistes*.

dalliance and set off for the wars. Ben Jonson wrote a poem with the title 'An Epistle to a Friend to persuade him to the Wars' which, oddly enough, contains the same word with the same sexual sense strongly suggested by innuendo:

> How much did stallion spend
> To have his court-bred filly there commend
> His lace and starch? And fall upon her back
> In admiration, stretched upon the rack
> At last, to him rich suit and title, Lord?

The sense seems still more clearly present in Jonson's 'Ode' ('If men, and times were now'): 'How soon with a self-tickling he was spent.'

Meanwhile Aristotle's point is that the civil authorities can relax; the emotions go away. In which case the poet may be permitted to stay in the city.

'The past is another country; they do things differently there.' Aristotle's thought is alien to us, perhaps even repellent. But it is odd how applicable it is to a mode of tragedy which he never saw and to a society which has, since his time, undergone not one but many transformations. In *our* world, people as they leave a football match are, quite clearly, in a different mental state from people leaving the theatre. Indeed the situation may be a degree odder than that. Readers of Allen Cameron's *Circus Factions: Blues and Greens at Rome and Byzantium* (Oxford: Clarendon Press, 1976) may wish to say, 'Actually, Aristotle's theory works *better* for our society than for the ancient world, since the hooliganism of the Blues and Greens was more closely linked to the theatre than to the Hippodrome.' But Cameron is dealing with the 4th and 5th centuries AD, a period as far in time from Aristotle as we are from Thomas Aquinas. Also, more importantly, the theatre of which Cameron writes was not tragic but pantomimic (quasi-pornographic), with organized claques providing a *simultaneous* spectacle of conflict in the auditorium.

Aristotle and Plato are united in their fear of emotion, or of the things which emotion can do. Stephen Halliwell makes the point strongly that there is no evidence at all to support the idea that pity and fear were considered morbid by Aristotle.[8] While emotion here need not be morbid, precisely, any more than bodily waste matter is morbid, it is quite clear that it is something we would wish to be rid of. Hence, indeed, the pleasure of the evacuation. Certainly, in other contexts (for example, *Nicomachean Ethics*, 1104 b 11–13, 1106 b 16–28, 1172 a 21 f.). Aristotle was willing to allow that rightly directed emotion could serve an ethical end. Here, however, the fear of emotion is evident.

I am similarly unpersuaded by Jonathan Lear's attempt to see *catharsis* as a mode of education and by Martha Nussbaum's presentation of it as a kind of clarification.[9] In that part of the *Politics* which introduces the notion of *catharsis*, Aristotle is worrying about flute-playing. He says in effect (and one can sense great arrogance of caste here) that no gentleman should play the flute *too well*, that it is better left to professionals (high-grade slaves); flute-playing, unlike other musical exercises, does not lead to an increase in intelligence but is rather a matter of dexterity (1341 a). Moreover, at *Politics*, 1341 a 21, he expressly contrasts the *catharsis* involved in such music with *mathesis*, 'learning'. This all falls within a general disparagement of flute-playing as emotional rather than ethical. *Catharsis* here, so far from being a mode of education, is almost seen as its opposite. The crucial passage, however, comes a page or so later at 1342 b 32 where Aristotle says that those 'subject to posses-

---

[8] *The Poetics of Aristotle* (London: Gerald Duckworth, 1987), p. 90 n. Cf. the same author's 'Pleasure, Understanding and Emotion in Aristotle's Poetics', in A. O. Rorty (ed.), *Essays on Aristotle's Poetics* (Princeton, New Jersey: Princeton University Press, 1992), pp. 241–60.

[9] Jonathan Lear, 'Katharsis', in A. O. Rorty (ed.), *Essays on Aristotle's Poetics*, pp. 315–40, esp. pp. 318–19; Martha C. Nussbaum, *The Fragility of Goodness: Luck and Ethics in Greek Tragedy and Philosophy* (Cambridge: Cambridge University Press, 1986), p. 389.

sion' (i.e. liable to, as to an illness, *katokochimoi*) by contact with music can be restored, through a continuation of 'enthusiastic' music, to tranquillity, *hosper iatreias tuchontas kai katharseos*, 'as if they had undergone medical treatment and catharsis'.

Yet commentators still resist the medical interpretation. G. F. Else, for example, says that we must not suppose that *catharsis* takes place in the spectator's soul; rather it is 'a process carried forward in the emotional material of the play by its structural elements, above all by recognition.'[10] Else's view is strongly moralized. For him, what is 'purified' is the tragic act of the protagonist, an act which is shown not to be morally *miaron* ('disgusting') because it turns out to have been performed in ignorance. This is a strange reading of Aristotle's sentence in the *Poetics* and seems still stranger to anyone who has just been reading the *Politics*. Phrases like 'the emotional material of the play' and 'structural elements' look like a fairly desperate attempt to pull the reader away from the obvious psychological reference of *pathemata* in Aristotle's Greek. Leon Golden singles out for special praise Else's claim that nothing in the text suggests that *catharsis* happens in the soul of the spectator.[11] In fact Aristotle's reference in the same sentence to 'pity and fear' takes us at once to the soul or psyche of the spectator (it is not Oedipus who feels pity: *we* pity *him*).[12] I suspect that Golden was covertly relying, rhetorically, on a 'knee-jerk' twentieth-century reaction against the word 'soul', a reaction which has arisen in response to a high-flown, religious implication in the word which formed well after the time of Aristotle. Later in the same article Golden, expounding his own view of *catharsis*, speaks of an improvement in our

[10] *Aristotle's Poetics: The Argument* (Cambridge, Mass.: Harvard University Press, 1957), p. 439.

[11] 'Catharsis', *Transactions of the American Philological Association*, vol. xciii (1962), pp. 51–60, at p. 52.

[12] Else tries to link *pathemata* to the feelings of the characters within the play (*Aristotle's Poetics: The Argument*, pp. 228–9).

understanding 'of the nature of pity and fear as they relate to the "human situation"'.[13] Here I wish, in my turn, to record my own 'knee-jerk' reaction against 'human situation'. It reeks of the twentieth century, is to my ear manifestly less promising as an explanatory term than 'soul', in this context. Golden has indeed placed the word in inverted commas but, to this reader at least, the implied apology is insufficient. This whole strange attempt to relocate *catharsis* inside the drama appears to stem from the work of Heinrich Otte, who said roundly in the 1920s that it is the events of the plot which are clarified.[14]

The short answer to all this is that *pathemata* which I, following instructions in the dictionary, rendered as 'emotions', does not mean 'events'. Aristotle has various words for the incidents of the drama, *epeisodia, ta sumpipta, pragmata*. I know of one place (not in Aristotle) where the word *pathemata* will bear the sense 'adventures'. Plato at *Republic*, 393 B writes *peri ton en Ithake kai hole Odusseia pathematon*, 'concerning the *pathemata* in Ithaca and in the whole *Odyssey*' (even here the word may be coloured by some sense of the passive, subjective experience of Odysseus: 'sufferings'). Such a secondary, 'objective' sense for the word needs to be signalled clearly by surrounding words, as it is in Plato's sentence. Otherwise *pathemata* will mean 'emotions', 'passions', things we suffer as distinct from things we do. Where 'pity' and 'fear' have already occurred in the sentence, the translation 'emotions' is doubly secure.

It might be said, however, that one element in Aristotle's sentence works against me. When he wrote *di' eleou kai phobou*, 'through pity and fear', even Ingram Bywater, who firmly backed the medical interpretation of *catharsis* as

---

[13] 'Catharsis', p. 57.
[14] See his *Neue Beiträge zur Aristotelischen Begriffsbestimmung der Tragödie* (Berlin: Weidmann, 1928), p. 10. See also Leon Golden, *Aristotle on Tragic and Comic Mimesis*, American Classical Studies, 29 (Atlanta, Georgia: Scholars Press, 1992), pp. 16–17.

acting upon the audience, had to allow that the phrase must mean something like 'through incidents arousing pity and fear' or 'by piteous and alarming scenes'.[15] Here, seemingly, pity and fear are being subjected to precisely the same 'objectification' of sense that I resisted in the case of *pathemata*. But even if we admit the word 'incidents' at this point, the link to pity and fear (especially the link to pity) makes the direction of Aristotle's thought clear. It is to the feelings of the audience, not to those of the characters; *pathemata* then works in the sentence as a means of bringing the matter home to the soul of the spectator. That indeed is why Bywater could translate as he did and at the same time continue without any difficulty to subscribe to the 'audience-purgation' theory of *catharsis*.

Leon Golden's own interpretation of *catharsis* is 'intellectual clarification'. This view, as we have seen, has been taken up since by Martha Nussbaum. To say that *catharsis* means 'clarification' is very like saying that *pathemata* means 'events': it *can* bear the meaning, in special contexts, but normally it does not. Nussbaum, writing in a note to her main text, says fairly modestly that while *catharsis* is linked with medical treatment, it is also linked to education.[16] This is already misleading in so far as it suggests that the two senses are evenly balanced. We may notice that here the pupil does not have the backing of the teacher, for Golden, Nussbaum's guide in matters to do with *catharsis*, actually concedes that *catharsis* in the sense of medical purgation 'would have been an easily and commonly understood term that would not require additional explanation'.[17]

In support of the sense 'clarification' Nussbaum, like Golden, cites important passages in the *Poetics* where Aristotle joins the pleasure of mimesis to the pleasure of

[15] *Aristotle on the Art of Poetry*, pp. 17 and 151.
[16] *The Fragility of Goodness*, p. 503, n. 18.
[17] 'The Clarification Theory of Catharsis', *Hermes*, vol. civ (1976), pp. 437–52, at p. 441.

learning (1448 b 13, 1448 b 15–17, with a cross-reference to *Rhetoric*, 1371 b 5 f.). Before this book is over I shall myself be concerned to rely heavily on this element in Aristotle's thinking. But we shall go wrong if we say, as Nussbaum begins to say, that in this process the emotions are themselves educated (as distinct from 'the emotions are purged away so that education can occur'). Nussbaum says that Golden was wrong to confine clarification to the intellect: Aristotle's view is 'more generous' . . . Clarification, for him, can take place *through* emotional responses, as the definition states.'[18] A page later she writes, 'Pity and fear are not just tools of clarification that is in and of the intellect; to respond in these ways is *in itself* valuable' (my italics).[19] In truth the notion of a tool is already too generous; the emotions are not the instrument of cleansing but the impurity which must be removed. Nussbaum sums up her position with these words: 'The function of tragedy is to accomplish, through pity and fear, a clarification (or illumination) concerning experiences of the pitiable or fearful kind. But that is, by a surprising piece of good luck, exactly what Aristotle has already said.'[20] That word 'exactly' is extraordinarily rash, coming as it does from such an experienced hand. For it is, precisely, not what Aristotle said.

I have already paused on the mildly problematic *di'*, 'through', in Aristotle's sentence ('through pity and fear'), conceding that it has a temporary effect of 'objectifying' the emotions, turning them into pitiable or fearful incidents. But Nussbaum has moved the position of that 'through' and made it govern *pathemata*, 'emotions', so that Aristotle is no longer speaking about '*catharsis* of emotions' but about something much more baffling, '*catharsis through* emotions'.

The whole clarification theory is offered almost as if the related passage in the *Politics* did not exist. Nussbaum says blandly, 'Golden does not discuss *Politics* 1341 b 32 ff.,

---

[18] *The Fragility of Goodness*, p. 390.   [19] Ibid., p. 391.   [20] Ibid.

which has sometimes been used to support the purgation view; nor shall I, in great detail.'[21] In fact, since Nussbaum wrote these words Golden has published *Aristotle on Tragic and Comic Mimesis*, in which he gives quite a lot of space to Bernays, and the *Politics* passage.[22] Even in the extended discussion, however, one receives the impression that the *Politics* passage is not so much dealt with as set aside. Bernays failed to notice, Golden says, that in the *Poetics* Aristotle was working 'on the basis of very different first principles'.[23] Of course Aristotle's thought has shifted, between the *Politics* and the *Poetics* but this does not mean that the earlier work is irrelevant to the later. Aristotle explicitly provides, in the *Politics*, a cross-reference to the still-to-be written *Poetics*. When he introduces the term *catharsis* at *Politics*, 1341 b 39 he tells the reader that his word 'will be explained later in my work on poetry'. Now while it is true that the promise of fuller explanation was not kept (unless in a lost 'second book' of the *Poetics*), it is evident that this part of the *Politics* was linked in Aristotle's mind with the *Poetics* and therefore cannot be set aside.

We have seen Martha Nussbaum suggesting, in a footnote, that the sense of 'clarification' is as prominent as the sense 'purgation'. In fact she is willing to argue on occasion that 'clarification' is the *dominant* sense—'the primary, ongoing, central meaning'.[24] Sometimes she seems to wish, as it were, to carry the argument into the midst of the enemy camp, by writing, first that 'the meanings "clearing up" and "clarification" will be appropriate and central ones for *Katharsis*' and then adding 'even in medical and ritual contexts'.[25] This looks like a bold stroke designed somehow to deprive me of my treasured passage in the *Politics*: even the obviously medical uses of *catharsis* are now to be seen not as counter-

[21] Ibid., p. 503, n. 18.
[22] *Aristotle on Tragic and Comic Mimesis*, pp. 6–12.
[23] Ibid., p. 7.
[24] *The Fragility of Goodness*, p. 389.
[25] Ibid., p. 390.

examples but as straightforward instances of the sense of 'clarification'. It is strategy which can be retorted upon the proponent. For (conversely) even those uses of *katharos* ('clean', 'pure', 'purged') and *katharsis* (*catharsis*) which are commonly cited to support the clarification theory actually presuppose that undesirable matter must be removed. For example Plato at *Phaedo* 66 D and 69 C–D associates *catharsis* with the intellectual development of the philosopher; Golden and Nussbaum accordingly cite these passages in support of their 'anti-purgation' line. But Plato is describing the development of intellect as a getting-rid of the body (*apallakteon autou*, 66 D). The same is true of *Republic*, 533 D where Plato speaks of the eye of the soul—but of the eye of the soul as being sunk in mud, *en borboro*.[26] Nussbaum herself writes that '*katharos* ['clarified'] recognition is what we have when the soul is not impeded by bodily obstacles'.[27] Here her own sentence suggests that there is matter to be removed. I will readily agree with Nussbaum that the idea of clearing up is present in medical contexts, if she in her turn will agree that the idea of getting rid of undesired matter is present in intellectual contexts. In fact she makes exactly this concession. Immediately after her claim, offered in support of Golden, that the 'central meaning' is one of 'clarification', she adds, 'i.e. of the removal of some obstacle, or dirt or obscurity'[28]—but she is, so to speak, unaware of the fact of concession.

It will be observed that Nussbaum and I are converging on a pretty simple idea of washing. When washing occurs something is cleaned and something is washed away. Do we then agree? No. Nussbaum's error is to misplace emotion in this scheme. She seems to think that the emotions are washed. In fact they are what is washed away, or purged. *They* are the obstacle, the dirt, the obscurity (or obscurers).

The real point rightly noted by Ingram Bywater is the

[26] Cited by Nussbaum, *The Fragility of Goodness*, p. 389.
[27] Ibid.   [28] Ibid.

grammatical status of the word *pathematon*, 'of emotions, taken with *katharsin*'. *Pathematon* is the genitive of *pathemata*. If this is a genitive denoting the object purged away or removed, then the emotions cannot be seen as in themselves good. The evidence that the genitive is indeed of this kind (as distinct from, say, '*catharsis*' [produced by] emotions') is abundant. Aristotle's repeated linguistic practice in comparable physiological passages confirms it and it is found frequently in other writers. Bywater cites numerous examples, among them Demosthenes speaking of a *catharsis* ('discharge') of blood—obviously not a discharge caused by blood —and Hippocrates referring to *catharsis* of saliva.[29] Most interestingly, Plato at *Phaedo*, 69 A (in a passage grievously ill-illustrated by R. S. Bluck)[30] actually speaks of *catharsis* of fear. The case meanwhile for the full, medical sense, 'purgation' remains strong. The parallel in the *Politics* is decisive.

For the Renaissance reader the whole passage would be invested with the 'antique' subjection of passion to reason, that is to say, with later Stoicism. Nor, since Stoicism itself is in part a simplification and in part a development of elements already present in Plato and Aristotle, is it, in my view, a wildly wrong-headed reading. Once we understand this we may begin to see the full originality of Sir Philip Sidney's *Defence of Poetry*, written near the end of the sixteenth century.

Sidney certainly knew the *Poetics* well. It is likely that, in the course of his visit to Italy (1574–5), he listened to Giacopo Zabarella, Professor of Logic at Padua, lecturing on the *Poetics*.[31] As a good Renaissance man Sidney was anxious to stress the continuity of his thought with that of the ancients and accordingly cites Aristotle at many points in the work. But with all his ingenuity he cannot conceal the fact

[29] *Aristotle on the Art of Poetry*, p. 156.
[30] See his translation (with commentary) of the *Phaedo* (London: Routledge and Kegan Paul, 1955), p. 55.
[31] See John Buxton, *Sir Philip Sidney and the English Renaissance* (London: Macmillan, 1964), p. 72.

that he liked emotion and considered the emotive power of poetry to be its greatest strength, rather than a temporary embarrassment. This divides him from Aristotle.

The psychic mechanics of Aristotle's anti-emotional theory remain elusive. Perhaps he never thought them through. But it looks as if the channelling-off of emotion depends upon a partial disjunction of poetry from reality. Poetry and rhetoric begin to move apart. The orator before a battle whips up the emotions of the soldiers for a real fight, which immediately follows. Aristotle's tragic poet, on the other hand, can hardly be said to cause the audience to do anything at all, once the performance is over. Auden's words, 'Poetry makes nothing happen', are profoundly Aristotelian.[32] Aristotle's poet certainly imitates the real world, but he does so in the hypothetical, not the categorical, mode. Unlike the historian who tells us 'what Alcibiades did' (1451 b 11), the dramatic poet tells us 'the kinds of things which would happen (*hoia an genoito*)' (1451 a 37–8)—deals with necessary and probable sequences rather than the actual. This causes the emotions to issue harmlessly upon vacancy, instead of being locked instantly into practical action. We must be careful not to mistake this for formalism. Aristotle could never be formalist as twentieth-century theorists are formalist. After all, his most famous theoretical bequest is the doctrine of *mimesis*, or representation. But he is very clear that a sequence of events, to be tragic, must be unreal.

Dr Johnson was never so thorough an Aristotelian as in his celebrated account of dramatic belief in the Preface to his *Shakespeare*:

It will be asked, how the drama moves, if it is not credited. It is credited with all the credit due to a drama. It is credited, whenever it moves, as a just picture of a real original; as representing to the auditor what he would himself feel, if he were to do or suffer what is there feigned to be suffered or to be done. The reflection that

[32] From 'In Memory of W. B . Yeats'.

strikes the heart is not, that the evils before us are real evils, but that they are evils to which we ourselves may be exposed. If there be any fallacy, it is not that we fancy the players, but that we fancy ourselves unhappy for a moment; but we rather lament the possibility than suppose the presence of misery, as a mother weeps over her babe, when she remembers that death may take it from her. The delight of tragedy proceeds from our consciousness of fiction; if we thought murders and treasons real, they would please no more.[33]

Obviously Johnson is at least partly right. If we thought that man dressed as Hamlet had really first stabbed and then forced poison down the throat of that other man dressed as Claudius, we would ring for the police. Johnson at the end of this paragraph makes this idea of hypothetical assent a precondition of tragic pleasure. It may be said that his reasoning is less than watertight. In particular he has, by the end of the paragraph, entirely forgotten his own example of the mother, who weeps at the thought that her child might die; surely this mother cannot *enjoy* her weeping, although it is clearly hypothetical grief? I am not sure whether Johnson would be shaken by such a remark, but it is in fact less crushing than it appears. It does not require the cynicism of a La Rochefoucauld or a Mandeville to perceive that a normal woman—not a morally depraved person— could *luxuriate* in such grief as she never could in the face of real, actual pain.

So far we have been seeking to attach a special significance to the mere fact of representation. However inertly mechanical, however mirror-like your scheme of representation, the representative sign must be distinguishable, as having a sign-like character, from the thing it signifies; or representation will not be perceived to have happened—

[33] 'Preface to Shakespeare', in *Johnson on Shakespeare*, ed. Arthur Sherbo, 2 vols., being vols. vii and viii of the Yale Edition of the Works of Samuel Johnson, 15 vols. (New Haven and London: Yale University Press, 1958–85), vol. vii, p. 78.

one would simply register a new arrival in the huge family of mere 'things'. As I have written elsewhere, 'You don't point at a cat with a cat; you use your finger, or a word.'[34] Realism and reality are entirely distinct. As J. L. Austin noticed, only false teeth can be realistic.[35] Austin's remote namesake, St Augustine asked, 'How could it be a true picture of a horse, unless it was a false horse?'[36] Intelligent people have always understood this point. But Aristotle, in any case, carries the argument a stage further. He expressly denies 'mirror realism' when he insists that the poet does not imitate the actual, but the probable.

Sidney, however, is clearly unhappy with all this. He wishes to close the gap between the orator addressing the army and the poet with his audience. The emotions stirred up by Sidney's poet are *motors of moral behaviour.* I do not know if David Hume ever read Sidney's *Defence.* Somehow it is hard to imagine him doing so. For all that, the seeds of Hume's famous inversion of Stoicism may be seen here. Hume wrote, 'Reason is and ought only to be the slave of the passions.'[37] This famous sentence not only inverts Stoicism, with its celebrated subordination of passion to reason; it also, as I hinted, inverts the Platonico-Aristotelian offensive against passion we noticed earlier. Hume's basic thought is very simple: an emotional revulsion from tyranny, say, may cause a person to resist, but the bare proposition 'Tyranny is wrong' will do nothing, until it is *felt.* Sidney is the first writer I know who says that the 'bodying forth' language of poetry, with its 'apparent shining',[38] is different from abstract prose ('that whereof the philosopher bestoweth but

---

[34] *A New Mimesis* (London: Methuen, 1983), p. 53.
[35] *Sense and Sensibilia* (Oxford: Clarendon Press, 1962), p. 72.
[36] *Soliloquies*, 11. x; in *Patrologia Latina*, ed. J.-P. Migne, vol. xxxii (Paris: 1845), col. 893.
[37] *A Treatise of Human Nature*, II. iii. 3, p. 415.
[38] *A Defence of Poetry*, in *Miscellaneous Prose of Sir Philip Sidney*, ed. Katherine Duncan-Jones and Jan van Dorsten (Oxford: Clarendon Press, 1973), p. 86.

a wordish description')[39]—though, predictably hints of the idea can be found in earlier rhetorical writers. Terry Eagleton, in a later age, will have none of this. He writes with fine scorn, 'It is less easy after Greimas and Genette to hear this clash of the rapiers in line 3.'[40] I do not share his confidence that we should rejoice to be so delivered. It is easy to smile with Eagleton as we read because he has picked a deliciously corny example; but is the underlying idea really to be thrown away? If we do so we are throwing away the special experiential character of poetic utterance, that which Sidney, seeing it separately for the first time, marvelled at. Indeed to throw it away would be to lose an obvious truth. For Sidney it is moral. The young Elizabethan, excited by reading about Aeneas, wants to be brave and dutiful, like him.

It may be thought that in claiming that Sidney is in favour of emotion I am in fact distorting him in the direction of my own wishes or tastes; that, while it is obviously true that Sidney believed that an image could prompt active emulation, he may well have thought, as a Renaissance Platonist, that the Good produced this effect automatically, without any involvement of human emotions. I grant that it is surprising that Sidney should favour emotion—and the more one knows about history the more surprising it becomes— and yet, I submit, it is so.

The *Defence*, to be sure, is not a grave philosophical treatise. Its own rhetorical status is ambiguous, somewhere between the *Poetics* of Aristotle and Erasmus's *Praise of Folly*, though in the long run nearer to the former than to the latter. Certainly there is about it a faint smell of conscious absurdity, of the tradition of the mock-encomium so congenial to the Renaissance (that is the tradition of praising something known to be despicable for the sheer fun of it, or else to display one's rhetorical ingenuity). But Sidney

---

[39] Ibid., p. 85.
[40] *Literary Theory: An Introduction* (Oxford: Basil Blackwell, 1983), p. 106.

really did love poetry and we can watch the argument becoming more and more urgent, behind the light elegance of the prose. I suspect that there existed in Sidney's mind a simple equation of poetry with delight, and 'delight' is of course the name of an emotion. It may be that the idea of delight at first led Sidney to conceive his 'Apology' as a work which would itself be the opposite of grave, but as he wrote he found that he wished, so to speak, to take delight seriously. He was obviously aware of the ancient theoretic oscillation between the poles of delight and instruction; it looks as if he was swiftly gripped by the thought that these are not opposites, that instruction might be better served by delight than by abstract gravity.

The *Defence* opens with an artful, half-humorous account of one John Pietro Pugliano, an esquire in the stable of the Emperor Maximilian II in Vienna, at whose court Sidney stayed in 1573. Pugliano is a joke, a walking specimen of prejudice incarnate who, because he is professionally involved with horses, thinks horsemanship the highest of all arts, the horse the noblest of animals. Sidney presents Pugliano as a comic example of reason ruled by emotion ('strong affection and weak arguments').[41] No sooner has he completed the picture of honest Pugliano, however, than he offers himself as a parallel. As Pugliano the horseman raved about horsemanship so he, Sidney the poet, will rave about poetry.

Only the coarsest of literary critics would conclude from this opening that we should simply regard all that follows as nonsense. Sidney like other good orators is master of the civil art of praising with faint damns. He offers himself as a kind of holy fool—'You will see that I'm emotionally involved in all this stuff'—secure in the knowledge that there's a level at which the confession will do him no harm at all— may even covertly raise his stock in the reader's mind.

[41] *A Defence of Poetry*, in *Miscellaneous Prose*, p. 73.

Similarly, when John Donne confesses to 'an hydroptique immoderate desire of humane learning',[42] the good reader knows, however much learned commentators may dredge up from Renaissance moralists concerning the Adamic sin of presumptuous curiosity, that Donne is not really ashamed of his appetite for learning, that he knows it renders him glamorous. Real, heartfelt confession sounds quite different. Sidney, I suspect, sensed that the time had come when he could count on an element of favourable feeling towards something which we, in the twentieth century, might call enthusiasm. He tells us that the old historians 'either stole or usurped of poetry their passionate describing of passions'.[43] Here the *word* 'passionate' is already beginning to work as praise rather than blame. So far, indeed, we have passion in the persons described and passion in the teller, but no passion in the hearer. It is evident, however, that Sidney regards strong feelings, present in the writing, as being mirrored in the reader's emotional reaction. He is likely to have had at the back of his mind the words of Horace. *Si vis me flere dolendum est / primum ipsi tibi:* 'If you want me to weep, you must first grieve yourself,' (*Ars Poetica*, 102–3). It is sometimes argued that because Horace formally addresses Telephus and Peleus, tragic personages, he is not at this point advising the poet but the actor— urging, in effect, a sort of 'method acting'. It seems to me that Horace never considers the emotions of the working actor; the context—and the title of the work—is the art of poetry. Horace modulates from a serious 'you', addressed to the poet, to a fanciful 'you', addressed to the poetic creation, Peleus or Telephus.

[42] *Letters to Several Persons of Honour* (London: printed by J. Flesher, 1651), p. 51; in Edmund Gosse, ed., *The Life and Letters of John Donne*, 2 vols. (London: Heinemann, 1899), vol. i, p. 191. Gosse prints 'human' where 1651 gives 'humane'.

[43] *A Defence of Poetry*, in *Miscellaneous Prose*, p. 75.

Sidney says of the Psalms of David,

what else is the awaking his musical instruments, the often and free changing of persons, his notable *prosopopoeias*, when he maketh you, as it were, see God coming in His majesty, his telling of the beasts' joyfulness and hills leaping, but a heavenly poesy, wherein almost he showeth himself a passionate lover of that unspeakable and everlasting beauty to be seen by the eyes of the mind, only cleared by faith?[44]

Here David is passionate and the reader, filled with David's poetry, is likewise impassioned. If the Idea of the Good simply operated by its own automatic power, it would be as strong in the pages of a philosophical treatise as it is in poetry. But that is precisely what Sidney denies. Only the poets offer 'the sweet food of sweetly uttered knowledge'.[45] The gustatory language is heavily emotive. Amid the glittering ingenuities of Sidney's *Astrophil and Stella* one line stands out by its power to convey elemental, elementary emotion: '"But ah", Desire still cries, "Give me some food".'[46] Sidney's continual harping about sweetness ('softened and sharpened with the sweet delights of poetry' and the like)[47] is a strategy evolved in express reaction against the rational method of the philosopher: 'I think that no man is so much *philophilosophos* ['a lover of the love of wisdom'] as to compare the philosopher in moving with the poet.'[48] Sidney rings the changes on the words 'teach' and 'delight': 'For these indeed do merely make to imitate, and imitate both to delight and teach; and delight, to move men to take that goodness in hand, which without delight they would fly as from a stranger . . .'[49] Here delight is no by-

[44] *A Defence of Poetry*, in *Miscellaneous Prose*, p. 77.
[45] Ibid., p. 80.
[46] Sonnet 71, in *The Poems of Sir Philip Sidney*, ed. William Ringler Jr. (Oxford: Clarendon Press, 1962), p. 201.
[47] *A Defence of Poetry*, in *Miscellaneous Prose*, p. 76.
[48] Ibid., p. 91.
[49] Ibid., p. 81.

product but an indispensable factor in that moral teaching which is special to poetry. 'Move', 'motion', 'emotion' are of course both etymologically and conceptually cognate.

Sidney is here speaking of the most exalted poets of old time. But even the lower sort of poetry can exert this motive/emotive power: 'Truly, I have known men that even with reading *Amadis de Gaule* (which God knoweth wanteth much of perfect poesy) have found their hearts moved to the exercise of courtesy, liberality, and especially courage.'[50] Notice that their hearts, not their minds are moved.

Notoriously, Sidney is forced by his moral stance to exaggerate the extent to which literature is peopled by ideally good figures, models. Where the Latin poet Horace, in a passage Sidney almost certainly knew says that Homer's *Iliad* teaches us the idiocy of bloody warlords (*quicquid delirant reges, plectuntur Achivi*: 'whatever madness the kings commit, the Greeks weep' (*Epistles*, 1. ii. 14), Sidney chooses to find nothing but luminous virtue in Achilles.[51] The effect on the notion of *mimesis* is spectacular. Sidney pays lip-service to the Aristotelian conception, but then pulls away, to say that really poets do not imitate the brazen world at all; rather, in a wild flight of ideal creativity, they give us a *golden* world. Here another of Aristotle's careful distinctions is being erased—for the *Poetics* begins with the presumption that, while everyone knows that poets are creative people (hardly avoidable for them since the Greek word for 'poet' means 'maker'), in fact all these poems are *not* straight 'makings', but are, at the same time, '*imitatings*'. Gilbert Murray wrote beautifully about the term 'imitate' as it appears in the second sentence of the *Poetics*. Bywater's translation of the Aristotle runs as follows: 'Epic poetry and tragedy, as also Comedy, Dithyrambic poetry, and most flute-playing and lyre-playing, are all, viewed as a whole, modes of imitation.' It is a sentence which simply washes

---

[50] Ibid., p. 92.　　　[51] Ibid., p. 86.

over the ordinary modern reader like so much soapy water. Murray pointed out that if we are to understand it we must be very simple and literal. Translating literally we get, 'Epic-making and the making of tragedy, as also Comedy and Dithyramb-making, and most flute-art and lyre-art are all, as it happens *imitatings.*'[52] Now that we have brought out the force of the reiterated word *poiesis*, 'making', the sentence begins to show a bit more point. The implied antithesis between making and imitating begins to come through. To make it extra-clear we could paraphrase thus: 'Tragedy-making and the rest are not simple makings but also imitatings.' Aristotle did not overlook the creative element in poetry; but he did insist on a certain modification. The archaic Greeks made war around the walls of Troy, but Homer made an imitation war of Troy. This sounds odd, I know, in English but it is less unnatural in Greek. In Greek the poet can be said to 'make a poem' but equally, Plutarch (ii. 105) can write of the poet as 'having made Achilles, speaking' (*poiesas ton Achillea legonta*). Because it is an imitation it is a poem, held in the verbal medium. It is called the *Iliad.* A Greek sculptor could make you *an* Athene but he could not make Athene. The sharpest illustration I know of this doctrine is the memorial at the corner of Hyde Park, near the Decimus Burton screen. It is in the form of a First World War field gun, executed in stone down to the last rivet. The sculptor has made a gun but he has not manufactured an armament. Its status as sculpture depends upon its being an imitation only; its realism depends upon its unreality. This particular piece fascinated me when I was a child, partly because I felt that some rule of the game was being broken. I suppose the straight lines and mathematical curves of the gun looked as if they might be susceptible of a mechanical—as distinct from an inexact, humane—replica-

---

[52] 'Poesis and Mimesis', in his *Essays and Addresses* (London: George Allen and Unwin, 1921), p. 108.

tion (odd to think of this sculptor as unsung predecessor of Andy Warhol, him of the soup-can . . .).

But Sidney is intent upon another enterprise. If he can arrange for his poet to drop representation and be once more a pure maker—of things better than this sorry world can provide—then imitation (as David Daiches saw)[53] *can be covertly transferred from the poet to reader.* For the kind of imitation Sidney likes is that performed by the thrilled reader, who tries to be like the heroes of the poets: no longer the poet imitating the world, but the reader imitating the poem.

It is odd that this kind of Mimesis is seldom noticed in modern discussions. Roughly speaking, two sorts of imitation are commonly mentioned: imitation or representation of the world and imitation by poets of previous poets. It might be thought that in this age of 'reader theory' the time is ripe for a revival of readerly mimesis. In a way, however, though the term 'mimesis' is missing, the idea is already to be found everywhere. The feminist critic who objects to the presentation of unacceptable female role-models is employing an essentially Sidneian theory of art.

Sidney is a central figure of the English Renaissance, if there ever was an English Renaissance. Milton, on the other hand, is a late-born man. For him the whole business of reviving antiquity is not, as one might have expected, made easy by long practice but is instead full of a sense of austere responsibility. He plays a minor part in the history of the interpretation of Aristotle's *Poetics,* but it is a curious one. I have already cited Milton, together with Minturno, in the honourable list of those who believe that *catharsis* means 'medical purgation', and I have cited the last line of *Samson Agonistes,* 'And calm of mind all passion spent' as a reference to *catharsis,* but all is not quite as simple as I have made it sound.

---

[53] *Critical Approaches to Literature* (London: Longman, 1956), p. 59.

In the preface to *Samson Agonistes*, 'Of that sort of Dramatic Poem which is called Tragedy', Milton wrote that the special power of tragedy was to 'temper and reduce [passions] to just measure with a kind of delight, stirred up by reading or seeing those passions well imitated'.[54] Quite clearly, Milton is remembering the doctrine of the moral and emotional mean as we have it in the *Nicomachean Ethics* (see especially 1106 b 16–23). This does not look like the 'medical purgation' theory at all but much more like ammunition for the other side. Predictably the words were seized on by Humphry House to support his ethical interpretation.[55] Unfortunately Milton offers no answer to the primary problem in this approach. Leon Golden writes, 'No purification theorist offers a mechanism by which *Katharsis* can cure *deficiency* of emotions.'[56] But Milton also wrote, in the same preface, that tragedy, a 'moral' and 'profitable' thing, is 'therefore said by Aristotle to be of power to purge the mind of those and such-like passions'. Then follows the clause about tempering the emotions, after which he returns to the medical reading: 'So in physic things of melancholic hue and quality are used against melancholy, sour against sour, salt to remove salt humours.'[57]

Given the subsequent history of Aristotelian commentary, Milton may be said to have hedged his bets very shrewdly indeed. It is as if he saw both Bernays and House coming. But, really, he cannot have it both ways. It looks—if later words cancel earlier—as if he settled on 'purgation'. The last line of *Samson Agonistes*, on the other hand, may be held potentially to support not House but Else. I have stuck firmly to the view that *catharsis* is something which happens not within the drama but to the spectators. Here, however, we have a pretty clear allusion to *catharsis* made not by the

[54] In *The Poems of John Milton*, ed. John Carey and Alastair Fowler (London: Longman, 1980), p. 343.
[55] *Aristotle's Poetics*, p. 110.
[56] *Aristotle on Tragic and Comic Mimesis*, p. 16.
[57] *The Poems of John Milton*, p. 343.

author in a preface but in the play itself, in application to the persons of the play. I said earlier that pity is not felt by Oedipus; rather *we* pity *him*—but Milton reminds us that there are people in tragedies who regularly feel pity: not the protagonist, to be sure, but the chorus. It is this perception which appears to have the effect of revising Else's notion that *catharsis* happens within the fabric of the play: *Samson Agonistes*, it will be said, both illustrates and asserts this fact.

I suspect that the last line of *Samson Agonistes* represents not the exclusion of *catharsis* from the audience that Else sought but a suggestion that there are times when audience response can cross the line dividing the auditorium from the stage, can invade the drama. *Catharsis* reappears within the play, not for Else's reasons, but precisely because the chorus are a kind of audience within the drama. They are more watchers than agents and *drama* (the Greek for 'doing') is concerned primarily with action.

Nevertheless there is something eerie in this nesting of *catharses*. 'Gaza mourns', the chorus tells us (1752), and we in our turn mourn too. We sense for a moment that the work is a mimesis of a mimesis, that we have witnessed not action simply but the *playing* of an action. Inside the story the final destructive feat of Samson is performed in a theatre (1605), it is a 'spectacle' (1604): 'In order to behold . . . the throng / On banks and scaffolds under sky might stand' (1609–10). Perhaps there is still enough Calvinism in Milton to make something in him believe that, at bottom, man is totally depraved and incapable of any great moral initiative. The heroes of Greek tragedies act, again and again, in defiance of jealous gods and are crushed for their rebellion. The most Samson can hope for is to be used by God: at the height of his heroism he remains an instrument only, a figure in the divine plan. There is a certain force in the jibe of the foolish Giant Harapha, that Samson would never have dared insult the great heroes of old had he not been armed in advance with supernatural magic (1130–4); 'At least *my* strength is my own', Harapha implies. The word *agonistes* in the title starts to resonate; behind the sense 'combatant' or 'champion', we begin to hear the sense 'leading player' (*protagonistes*). The word *agonistes*, without any prefix, is used to mean 'actor' in the pseudo-Aristotelian *Problemata* at 918 b 28. The austere, consciously primitivist plot of *Samson Agonistes* is in a way dynamized by a self-reflexive tremor. It is a play-within-a-play, but one of the plays was written by God, who writes using real people. 'Calm of mind all passion spent': meanwhile '*catharsis*' refers, still, to *audience* psychology.

2

ENTER FREUD

Sidney transformed *mimesis*, quietly shifting it from the poet to the excited reader, who emulates and copies the great figures of ideal art. But we cannot leave the matter there. Sidney also revived Platonist theory in such a way as to cancel a modification carefully introduced by Aristotle. It is a restoration which involves a considerable irony.

I have said that Sidney changed the nature of the poet, turned Aristotle's copyist of probabilities back into a free-ranging creator or maker. I use the designedly brutal word 'copyist' in order to acknowledge the element of mere imitation which really is involved. But as soon as we say 'of probabilities' we are requiring the exercise of intelligent imagination. That is why Aristotle thought poetry was 'more philosophical' (1451 b 5) than a mere chronicle of events. Now this account of Sidney's poet as moralist creator holds good as long as we take reality to be constituted by the available world. But Plato, as everyone knows, believed this world to be a tissue of inadequacy, while true reality lay beyond, in an ideal realm.

Plato works outwards, from inner implications of the word *know*. When we say, 'Jane knows that the murder rate in South Africa is high', we imply, immediately and 'tightly', that the murder rate in South Africa is in fact high. One can *know* only that which is the case. Of course a person can claim to know something which is later found not to have been the case, but the effect of the discovery is simply to show what purported to be knowledge was not really knowledge at all. It is true that recent years have seen the growth of a special idiomatic use of *know*, which conflicts with what I have just said: 'I just *know* I'll win', says the boxer, the night before the fight. Here 'know' cannot be linked directly to what is the case. He does not mean, for example, 'I know this because I have just administered a fatal poison to my opponent.' 'Know' here must mean, in cash terms, something like 'I am convinced that'. The conceptual shift is usually betrayed by an inflection of the voice, an emphasis. Once the rhetorical character of the idiom is fully discerned, it is innocuous enough, but, before that stage is reached, it is reasonable to feel that the speaker is incurring a kind of unacknowledged overdraft, drawing illicit support for his claim from the epistemologically powerful term, *know*, despite its inapplicability to the present situation. We wish to answer, indignantly, '*How* can you *know* that?' G. K. Chesterton, on the other hand, makes interesting use of the old, central implication of *know* when he makes Adam Wayne in *The Napoleon of Notting Hill* answer the suggestion that God, who made the world, may know it is all a hideous joke. 'He could not know it,' says Wayne, 'for it is not a joke.'[1] We, who live in the world, know this.

Given, then, that we can know only that which really *is*, Plato (the great natural enemy of Locke, born centuries later) is struck by the weakly fluctuating character of presentation; what is immediately given to our senses is always inchoate or in decay, variable and imperfect. This, clearly, is not what we *know*. A mind which inertly received, in endless series, these fluctuations would know nothing; of themselves the fluctuations cannot build knowledge. Therefore Plato decided that knowledge is grounded in what he called the ideas, or Forms, which stand on the far side of presentation. The word *idea* can easily mislead the modern reader who will instantly think of some mental object. For Plato (who explicitly denied that Ideas are thoughts)[2] the Idea is

---

[1] V. iii (Harmondsworth: Penguin Books, 1946), p. 155.
[2] *Parmenides*, 132 B–C.

not interior but rather as it were *further out*, more truly objective than the field of experience. In other words, for Plato 'ideal' and 'real' are not opposed terms but are fused. Much of our mental life, however, is infected by the fluctuations of the sensuous medium. We are not now as once we were.

Sidney the Renaissance Platonist is heir to this conception of reality as ulterior or transcendent. This means in effect that the Sidneian picture of the poet freely ranging within the zodiac of his own wit to *create* a golden world can now be re-construed: if this given world is alone real then indeed the poet's world will appear fictive, freely invented; but if the ideal is itself the sole reality, the golden world of the poets may be, after all, a just picture, a faithful mimesis, of that transcendent reality. But Sidney is also a Christian and so the Platonic world of Ideas receives a strongly ethical colouring, in partial contrast with the severely epistemological view of the Greek philosopher. I have said that *idea* in the post-classical world was psychologized and given the meaning, 'mental object'. Meanwhile of course the *adjective* has been *moralized*: *ideal* now means 'very good'. That is why on those occasions when Sidney does make use of Aristotelian mimesis, he tends to transform Aristotle's probable 'would' into a moral 'should'. Sidney's poet shows us not what would happen but what should or ought to happen.[3] This morally ideal world will be seen *sub specie temporis* as unreal (in which case the poet who depicts it will be a *fictor*, a feigner), but *sub specie aeternitatis* it is of course the only real one. The epistemological 'Fall' from true original knowledge represented in Plato's theory of ideas is in some ways reflected in the Christian story of the loss of Paradise. Sidney was arguing the case for poetry with Protestants who believed that human capacity was totally depraved by the Fall. The severer doctors of the Reformation

[3] See Daiches, *Critical Approaches to Literature*, p. 65. Aristotle allowed that Sophocles depicted men 'as they ought to be' (*Poetics*, 1460 b 34).

are clear that not only our moral impulses but our intellectual powers are depraved and incapacitated by the Fall.
Calvin affirmed that science was by gift of God, 'The spirit
of God is the sole fountain of truth',[4] and George Herbert
wrote, 'We say amisse / This or that is: / Thy word is all, if
we could spell' ('The Flower'). Calvin admittedly seems to
hesitate when, at *Institutes*, II. ii. 12, he concedes common-
sensically that man, totally depraved though he is, clearly
has enough reason remaining in him to distinguish him from
the brute creation. But within a few pages he makes it clear
that every time a pagan philosopher said something true,
every time a sinner correctly adds two and two, it is God
who does these things. One might react by saying, 'But this
is glorious, it shows what God-filled creatures we are, since
we are continually getting sums right! Might not our poetry
and art be similarly God-filled?' To this one must answer,
'Perhaps, but Calvin would never have it so.' The complete
worthlessness of human powers, moral and intellectual, continues to dominate his mind. Poetry, certainly, has nothing
to do with God, everything to do with human depravity, in
Calvin's scheme of things. When Sidney writes that the poet
has a fallen will but an erected wit[5] he is making an auda-
cious claim—for a kind of unfallen clairvoyance in ideal art,
'the imposition cleared, hereditary ours'.[6] In the same sentence, he speaks of poetry as working 'with the force of a
divine breath'. Here the word 'inspiration' is brought back
to (dangerous) life—'dangerous' because Sidney is here referring unequivocally not to pagan divinities but to God,
'the heavenly maker' of the maker. It might be thought that
the effect of the notion of Christian inspiration is to recon-
cile Sidney's position with Protestant total depravity of man
since it is now God who writes the poetry, but Sidney's

---

[4] *Institutes of the Christian Religion*, ed. J. T. McNeill and F. L. Battles, 2
vols. (London: SCM Press, 1961), vol. i, p. 273.
[5] *A Defence of Poetry*, in *Miscellaneous Prose*, p. 79.
[6] Shakespeare, *The Winter's Tale*, I. ii. 75.

allusion to the poet's 'erected wit' obstinately suggests that, somehow, the human agent is admitted to the vision of perfection. Either way the claim is that we find in poetry a prelapsarian glory. I suspect that the claim is so bold that Sidney frightened himself a little when he made it, for at this point he stalls, and retreats to what he calls 'the more ordinary opening' of the poet as imitator. He was relatively safe as long as he stayed with the alternative language of antiquity, speaking not of Paradise but of a golden world.[7] Either way, the poet is here, once more, no unconstrained creator but rather an imitator of reality, though now the reality is transcendent. It is a story which was to be repeated in later Romantic literary theory. Think of the way the word 'Imagination', the free-ranging word, is intermittently replaced in Blake's writings by the cognitive word, 'Vision' —the poet as copyist of eternity (an unwritten poem by Wallace Stevens?).

I have said that this particular restoration of Platonism is deeply ironic. Plato himself, you see, would have been on the side of the Calvinist enemies of poetry. For him, if the available world was *once* removed from reality, the artist who initiates an invitation is *twice* removed (*Republic*, 597 E), doubly mendacious (those who turn up the passage in the Greek will find that Plato actually says not 'doubly' but 'triply', but this seems to be simply an example of Greek 'inclusive counting'—for an ancient Greek Thursday would be not two but three days after Tuesday). Remember that Aristotle's *Poetics* is an apology for poetry, written against the Puritan in Plato. Yet we call Sidney Platonist. This is because the structure set up by Plato virtually invites a certain adjustment, which Sidney was in due course to exploit against the Puritans of his own day. The neo-Platonist Plotinus affirmed that the poet is not doubly removed from the ideal but, on the contrary, has the power to re-ascend to

---

[7] *A Defence of Poetry*, in *Miscellaneous Prose*, p. 78.

the prior Ideas.[8] Here Plato's 'fall' is cancelled just as surely as Calvin's 'total depravity' is cancelled in Sidney's phrase, 'erected wit'.

The Platonic line in critical theory is the exciting one. The godlike artist whose solar gaze burns through accident to reach essence, the redemptive vision, and so on—these thoughts will probably always be, if not inspiring, inspiriting. But the problem of tragedy is a reef upon which all but the strongest ships break up. By this ancient test the neo-Platonic line, with its easy fusion of imagination and reality, fails, while the quieter—I want to say the *truer*—Aristotelian version survives. Sidney's theory in its most frequently stated form requires a literary universe of golden heroes. That the contemplation and excited emulation of such beings should be pleasurable will surprise no one. True, only a trifling adjustment of the theory is required to permit the appearance of wicked characters—that is by introducing the *negative* role-model, the person whose behaviour is so manifestly vile that we all strive to behave differently. There may be, so to speak, a converse ideality of wickedness. Sidney makes the adjustment, when he writes of 'a niggardly Demea' and 'a vainglorious Thraso'.[9] But do not be misled by my phrase 'converse ideality' into thinking that he is in any degree engaged with the morally tense field of tragedy. What he wants is 'poetic justice', and poetic justice is one of the first casualties of tragedy.

But if the Platonic theory is unduly exalted, the Aristotelian, it might be said, is almost grotesquely debased. For is not Aristotle saying that the pleasure of tragedy is the pleasure of vigorous excretion? Aristotle in the *Poetics*, it could be claimed, is a little like Swift on the Aeolists in *A Tale of a Tub*, where spirit itself is turned into the grossest matter by

---

[8] *Enneads*, V. viii. i, in *Plotinus*, with an English translation by A. H. Armstrong, Loeb Classical Library, 7 vols. (London: Heinemann, 1966–88), vol. v (1984), p. 238.

[9] *A Defence of Poetry*, in *Miscellaneous Prose*, p. 96.

being turned into (what is after all its etymological origin) wind (eructations and the like), with remarkable consequences for the doctrine of inspiration. But while, for Swift, all this was a joke, Aristotle is quite serious. There is some force in the charge, but only some. Aristotle's theory of *catharsis* really is founded on a digestive model, but it is not a reductive physicalist theory.

Certainly the picture we have so far suggests some sort of reference to the Greek theory of bodily humours, despite the fact that humour theory is virtually absent from the *Nicomachean Ethics*, Aristotle's principal treatise on moral and social psychology. It is clear that for all his dislike of physiological reduction, Aristotle did sometimes think in terms of humours. Martha Nussbaum, anxious to scotch physicalism, points out that the full theory is found only in the *Problemata*—and the *Problemata* is not by Aristotle, though it was once thought to be his. The *Problemata* seems to be a post-Aristotelian product of the school he founded, the Peripatetics, and it is commonly agreed that the later Peripatetics were increasingly materialist.[10] This move towards materialism, however, may not have been a simple addition to (or a subtraction from) the thought of the master; it is quite conceivable that it represents a coarsening or literalizing of Aristotle's own analogical reflections. Even in the *Nicomachean Ethics* we can occasionally find him thinking in terms of humours. At 1154 b 9–20 he does so in association with purgative pleasure (it looks very much as if he is thinking of music, as it is described in *Politics*). Leon Golden seizes triumphantly on the passage as vindicating his view that *catharsis* in the *Poetics* cannot be medical, on the oddly technical ground that Aristotle here describes curative pleasures as 'accidental', while in the *Poetics*, *catharsis* is used to describe the essential character of mimesis.[11] The argument is indeed fine-drawn. There may

[10] See A. E. Taylor, *Aristotle* (London: Methuen, 1964), p. 13.
[11] *Aristotle on Tragic and Comic Mimesis*, p. 11.

be mild contradiction in Aristotle's suggesting, in one place, that therapeutically purgative pleasure is essential to normal enjoyment of tragedy and, in another (the *Nicomachean Ethics*), that such purgative pleasures are accidental in the sense that they apply only to special cases of imbalance. But such wobbles are common in the thought of any working philosopher. What is really striking is the undoubted fact that when he speaks of curative pleasures he begins to think about humours. He says explicitly that those who suffer from an excess of black bile are in torment because of the special mixture of humours in them (1154 b 11–13).[12] Nevertheless those who insist that the theory of *catharsis* offered in the *Poetics* is unlikely to be an instance of full physicalism remain correct. I do not believe that Aristotle is offering a Galenic account of emotions as physical humours, requiring actual excretion from time to time. Rather he is proposing an analogy: as the body seeks to ease its load of waste matter, so the soul—the higher faculty if you like terms of value—seeks to ease its burden of emotion. That is why, apparently against all the odds, the audience leaving the theatre after *Oedipus Rex* feels relief. What they have seen is terrible; what they feel is a kind of ease. This is not simply a feeling of relief that the suffering has stopped. Rather, the relief is integrated with the full process of the drama, with the complete discharging of the tragic sequence from beginning to end.

It is sometimes said that scholarly literary theories can never be predictive as scientific theories are predictive, because literary texts naturally belong to the past. But the accumulations of the past are so rich that our knowledge of them is incomplete, variable, and subject to innovation. One

[12] The point is suppressed in W. D. Ross's standard translation of the *Nicomachean Ethics*. He renders Aristotle's *melagcholikoi* ('those having an excess of black bile') simply as 'people of an excitable nature', but does supply an explanatory footnote. Earlier, at 1150 b 25, we have exactly the same suppression, this time with no footnote. See *The Basic Works of Aristotle*, ed. Richard McKeon (New York: Random House, 1941), pp. 1057 and 1049.

can therefore make predictions of the form, 'If you look you will—or will not—find *x*.' For example, 'Jane Austen's novels exhibit a certain empirical modesty; this means that you will never find two male persons talking without a female being present.' I will not say whether this particular prediction survives; I merely offer it as the kind of prediction that can be made. Aristotle's theory is so anciently familiar that it is hard to see the predictive charge it must once have carried. When the *Poetics* was first delivered, those who listened would have received an intellectual invitation to *go and look*, that is to check their own theatrical experience at the next opportunity. 'You will find', the prediction ran, 'that the experience will, as it were, "taste of" relief.' This check can be made again today, and verification obtained.

If Aristotle's theory is not physicalist, it is not formalist either. If the world with its griefs and terrors were not represented the emotions would not be activated—and they must be activated before they are discharged. Aristotle allows a separable, prior pleasure in the mere *reading* of a mimetic representation, the simple process of the learning what is here being represented (1448 b 13). But, equally, the representation must not fuse with actuality or our tragic pity would lead to our rushing on to the stage to comfort the protagonist, our tragic fear to flight from the theatre. I was careful to say earlier that even one-to-one mimesis of the actual involves the formal independence—the 'non-reality' —of the signifier, and to add that Aristotle's conception is in any case not of a one-to-one 'mirror-mimesis', but proposes the interposition of a further space, making mimesis hypothetical. One wonders what Aristotle would have said about portrait painting: perhaps that our pleasure becomes truly aesthetic only when it is rendered hypothetical by the death of the subject. It is striking that our inability to check the photographic accuracy of Rembrandt's self-portraits does not *begin* to impair, it would seem, our ability to respond to them as great art. But—Aristotle would swiftly add—we crucially need nevertheless to know what *faces* can be like in order to understand how humanity can glisten in the thickening of the paint. Because we inhabit a causal continuum we can speak of *real* probabilities, and that is why it is possible for an art which treats no actual existent to deal nevertheless with the world we all inhabit. Drama is something simultaneously real and unreal, real at the level of probability, unreal at the level of actuality (the medieval scholastic terms would be 'act' and 'potency').

I would add that the continuous, inter-related, causally impregnated character of reality is in any case presupposed at all times by our use of common nouns and general terms. Empiricism has always had an inner tendency to confine reality to a mere series of existents—hence the movement in the seventeenth century to reform language in the direction of a (wholly useless) litany of proper nouns. But the Brutus in Shakespeare's *Julius Caesar* is not the historical Brutus. Rather, he shows us what a certain kind of Stoic would do. The interesting thing is that language allows us to reformulate that last thought in apparently categorical terms —something like 'Shakespeare gets Stoicism right' (replacing the falsifiable, 'Shakespeare gets the historical Brutus right'). Here a categorical statement, pitched at a high level of generality, will be found to depend on hypotheticals at a lower level: getting Stoicism right will be found to be identical with 'saying what a Stoic would do'—as distinct from 'saying what Brutus did'.

Aristotle's decision to locate mimetic art in the hypothetical rather than the categorical mode I take to be an act of philosophic genius. The thought is in itself very simple— one of those thoughts which is as it were too large and simple to be easily taken in. In this quality of simplicity it resembles Hume's similarly fundamental critique of induction and causality, which is far less complex in its structure than are the mental processes gone through every evening by persons playing darts in pubs. Of course, in one way Hume is the opposite of Aristotle. The great difference is that Aristotle's notion enables us to make sense of what we all do, while Hume's thought is challengingly destructive. The famous phrase *hoia an genoito*, 'the kinds of things that would happen' (1451 a 37), works through a robust confidence in induction; for Hume, who could see in the fact that the sun has always risen no reason whatever to believe that it will rise tomorrow, the phrase 'what would happen' could not connote a relation to reality. To this day apologists for critical formalism habitually write as if mimesis were a theory of one-to-one correspondence of art and actuality. Aristotle may be held to have some rights in this word, and he certainly meant something else.

The theory that tragic pleasure consists not in some conscious re-construing of apparently desolating actions but in a psychic discharge, the process of which is not noticed though its consequence is felt—this, I submit, takes us some of the way. It really does explain why pleasure might be possible for people watching a tragedy. But Aristotle set himself a stiff task with the self-imposed phrase *oikeia hedone*, 'the proper pleasure' (1453 b 11), and I think that though he out-distanced Plato, he did not finally meet the challenge he set himself. He showed how tragic pleasure is possible but not exactly why it happens in a given case. If the pleasure is simply that of eased emotions and the pleasure is in practice initially contested at the conscious level by distressing emotions such as pity and fear, why do we not go for an uncontested discharge—say of emotions like hope or greed? Indeed, wish-fulfilment drama would seem to offer simultaneous gratification and *catharsis* (release of excess pressure). Of course if there were an unstoppable welling-up of fear in all of us which simply required expulsion from time to time, recourse to the tragic theatre would be explained: this theatre for that *catharsis*, the other theatre for the other. But Aristotle, despite his use of the alimentary analogy, is unlikely to have believed this.

The person who did believe something of this sort is Sigmund Freud. At least, Freud believed in quasi-physiological cathexes of psychic force—in psychic *quanta*—requiring periodic discharge. It will be noticed that I am already employing 'hedging' terms like 'quasi-physiological'. It seems that anyone who seeks to explain the thought of Aristotle or of Freud is obliged to sooner or later acknowledge that, despite early suggestions of an earthy simplicity, the theory cannot be understood in exclusively physical terms. With both thinkers we find ourselves in a psychophysical limbo. Nevertheless, that said, they face, so to speak, in opposite directions. Aristotle is consciously opposed to physical reduction; Freud is temperamentally drawn to it. Martha Nussbaum's opposition to the medical interpretation of *catharsis* flows partly from a well-founded sense of this side of Aristotle; she writes, 'Aristotle's work on psychological processes announces its opposition to physiological reductionism in no uncertain manner.'[13] It looks as if Nussbaum is briskly assuming that to give a medical sense to *catharsis* is to be committed immediately to full physicalism, with no possibility of a less constrained, analogical application of the term.

In the early 1870s Freud fell under the influence of Emil Du Bois-Reymond, Ernst Brücke, and Hermann Helmholtz, who joined forces in a robust refusal to make use of anything outside 'the common physical-chemical forces' or 'the physical-mathematical method', scorning vitalism, metaphysics, mysticism.[14] This hard, positivistic stand in Freud's conception of his own work persisted to the end of his life. In the *New Introductory Lectures on Psychoanalysis* of 1932 Freud rejected the idea that psychoanalysis was a

[13] *The Fragility of Goodness*, p. 502, n. 17.
[14] See Peter Gay, *Freud: A Life for Our Time* (London: Macmillan, 1988), p. 34.

philosophy proposing a *Weltanschauung* or 'world-view' of its own; on the contrary it is, he wrote, merely 'a part of science'.[15] In *The Outline of Psychoanalysis*, written in the last year of his life, he distinguished his own practice from earlier investigations which had been confined to the field of consciousness: psychoanalysis, he observed with quiet satisfaction, through its investigation of unconscious forces, was able 'to take its place as a natural science like any other'.[16]

Of course Freudian psychology turns out to contain many elements which resist translation into physical terms. In his paper, 'The Unconscious', Freud shows himself to have been aware of many of the problems involved. The very term 'Unconscious' suggests mindless forces or materials, and the fundamental idea that the Unconscious is actually made of repressed matter, of materials which are unacceptable to the conscious mind, seems to enforce this 'anti-mental' model. Freud says that in the Unconscious there is 'no negation, no doubt, no degrees of certainty', but 'only contents', connected with greater or lesser strength.[17] At the same time, however, he has to concede that these 'contents' may be emotions and that it is surely 'of the essence of an emotion that we should be aware of it'. It is impossible to avoid, he says, 'the strange conjunction, "unconscious consciousness of guilt", or a paradoxical "unconscious anxiety"'.[18] The privative prefix 'Un-' is appropriate, it would seem, as long as we consider the Unconscious from the (occluded) perspective of the ordinary conscious mind. In its own terms it is a second field of consciousness—an

[15] *New Introductory Lectures on Psychoanalysis*, in *The Complete Psychological Works of Sigmund Freud*, translated from the German under the general editorship of James Strachey, 34 vols. (London: Hogarth Press, 1966–74), vol. xxii (1964), p. 181.
[16] *Complete Psychological Works*, vol. xxiii (1964), p. 158.
[17] In *Papers on Metapsychology*, *Complete Psychological Works*, vol. xiv (1957), p. 186.
[18] Ibid., p. 177.

'Infra-conscious' rather than an Unconscious. Pascal's remark is strangely appropriate: 'Le coeur a ses raisons que la
raison ne connaît point' (*Pensées*, iv. 277): the Unconscious
has a mind of which Mind is wholly unaware. Freud's suggestion that 'mentalist' elements like negation and uncer-
tainty are introduced only as a result of censorship,
operating between the Preconscious and the Unconscious
does little to clarify the issue.[19] We are not, after all, conscious of the fact that we repress, or of the process of repression; all this has to be explained to us by Freud. But in that
case it would seem best to confess that repression is simply
an unconscious process and that, in consequence, the Unconscious contains, in addition to the repressed matter/
drives/emotions, a repressive agent, a kind of policeman in
the criminal underworld. Freud's word 'between' is a desperate shift, an attempt to find in intermediacy a means of
disguising contradiction. No middle ground is actually
established; instead the mere notion of mediation is invited
to stand in for the fact. It is all curiously reminiscent of
Descartes's notorious attempt to explain how unextended
mind could act upon extended matter through intermediate
'animal spirits'.

Certainly the radical physicalism of Du Bois-Reymond,
Brücke, and Helmholtz is hard to square with the ubiquit-
ously purposive character of Freud's Unconscious. Because
the primary motions of the Id are goal-directed they can be
described as wishes, and it is hard to see how any arrange-
ment of atoms or molecules, *qua* atoms or molecules, can be
said to form a wish. J. B. S. Haldane once wrote that he
could see how motions of atoms in his brain could be sound
chemically but he could not see how he could infer from
such chemical soundness that they were also sound logically;[20] in other words, thoughts can be accurate or true, but

---

[19] *Complete Psychological Works*, vol. xiv, p. 186.
[20] 'When I am Dead', in his *Possible Worlds* (London: Chatto and Windus,
1930), p. 209.

it is hard to see how a set of physical bits and pieces, however complex, can ever be true (Haldane, to be sure, withdrew the argument later).[21] In a similar way, we could ask, 'How can a quantum of matter *of itself* seek libidinal satisfaction?'.

'But what about Darwinism?' someone might say. Darwin's critique of teleological biology is the most important move against purposiveness the world has ever seen; the 'argument from design', the notion that organisms adapt *intelligently* to the environment, is unequivocally rejected. Yet Darwinians, among friends, regularly permit themselves purposive terminology: the giraffe's long neck, they say, is there *in order that* it may reach food placed high above the ground. If 'hard' Darwinians do this, why can't Freud? But Darwinians who speak in this way do so from a secure consciousness that their language is metaphorical. The apparent references to purpose are clearly understood as a sort of retrospective short-hand. 'The giraffe's neck is for reaching' means only 'the giraffe's neck (after long elimination of shorter-necked animals) functions in practice as a means of reaching'. The pattern of usage is possible only because of the clear, separate existence of long necks, a certain ecological niche, a certain evolutionary history. But in the case of Freud's Unconscious there is no such separate physical entity or process which can be construed analogically as a wish; the libidinal motion *is* a wish.

Peter Gay, in his biography of Freud, says that Freud's 'mechanistic metaphors, "neurons", "quantity", "biological rules of attention and defense" and the rest' were instilled in him by his early medical training.[22] In a way the most important word here is 'metaphors', though Gay seems to be unaware of the fact. For, as long as these terms remain metaphorical and not literal, Freud is no physicalist (and vitalism, we might add, is alive and well). But Freud

[21] 'I Repent an Error', *The Literary Guide*, 7 and 29 April, 1954.
[22] *Freud: A Life for Our Time*, p. 79.

certainly *tried* to think physically about the psyche. There is a place in the *Introductory Lectures on Psychoanalysis* where he is clearly annoyed by the 'mentalist' implications of the term 'traumatic' and hastily seeks to assimilate it to a species of somatic economics: 'The term "traumatic" has no other sense than an economic one.'[23] Within a few lines he moves from the economic model to the notion of an energizing stimulus (as if a trauma were some kind of electric shock). Either way he is struggling to preserve those elements which seem most surely to render the field amenable to scientific investigation and control.

We in the late twentieth century tend to see Freud as a great, dubious myth-maker; his contemporaries, after the initial shock of the material, often saw him as a hard, reductive scientist, dragging down the human spirit. When Virginia Woolf reviewed J. B. Beresford's *An Imperfect Mother* for *The Times Literary Supplement* (25 March 1920), her piece was entitled 'Freudian Fiction'. Her general attitude to Freud is one of tensely conceded respect for its scientific credentials together with an insistence that such science can only impoverish the human: 'The triumphs of science are beautifully positive', she writes, 'But for novelists the matter is much more complex . . . Yes, says the scientific side of the brain, that is interesting; that explains a great deal. No, says the artistic side of the brain, that is dull and has no human significance whatever.'[24] Bernard Shaw professed that he had originally supposed that a scientific psychology was impossible (because of the indecent, sexual element) but was persuaded by the example of Freud that it was after all possible.[25] D. H. Lawrence's hostility to Freud is well known: 'Freudianism is only a branch of medical

[23] *Complete Psychological Works*, vol. xvi (1963), p. 275.
[24] *The Essays of Virginia Woolf,* ed. Andrew McNeillie, 4 vols. (London: Hogarth Press, 1986–), vol. iii (1988), pp. 196–7.
[25] See his letter to Emil Ludwig, 13 February 1948, in Bernard Shaw, *Collected Letters*, ed. Dan H. Lawrence, 4 vols. (London: Max Reinhardt, 1965–88), vol. iv, *Collected Letters 1926–50* (1988), p. 814.

science.' These words, taken from a letter to Gordon Camp-
bell,[26] echo Freud's, but when Lawrence is the writer the
effect is to condemn. In *Psychoanalysis and the Unconscious* he allowed his language to become more explicit: 'the
machine-plan and the machine-principles of an automatized
psyche'.[27]

It is with Lawrence that the irony of the whole situation
begins to be apparent. For, whatever Freud's hopes, he
simply was not the hard experimentalist imagined by
Lawrence. Karl Popper's querying the testability of a large
area of psychoanalytic theory[28] together with such
devastating attacks as that by Wolpe and Rachman on the
'Oedipus Complex'[29] have left us with a Luciferan figure, a
fallen angel of natural science who still has power to haunt
the imagination. D. H. Lawrence was savaging a fellow
artist.

But the ethical opposition between the artist Lawrence
and the artist Freud remains. Freud, like some Stoic of
antiquity, sought to control the anarchic under-elements in
human nature, while Lawrence sought no such thing. Freud
saw himself as not only the investigator but also the heroic
antagonist of the Unconscious. In the *New Introductory
Lectures on Psychoanalysis* he affirmed that the goal of the
psychoanalysis was 'to strengthen the ego': 'Where id was,
there ego shall be. It is a work of culture—not unlike the
draining of the Zuider Zee.'[30] Some nine years earlier he

[26] 21 September 1914, in the Cambridge Edition of *The Letters of D. H.
Lawrence*, general editor James T. Boulton, 7 vols. (Cambridge: Cambridge
University Press, 1979–93), vol. ii (1981), p. 218.
[27] (London: Martin Secker, 1931), pp. 125–6.
[28] See especially 'Philosophy of Science: A Personal Report', in *Philosophy
in the Mid-Century*, ed. C. A. Mace (London: George Allen and Unwin, 1957),
pp. 151–91; reprinted (with altered title) in Karl Popper, *Conjectures and
Refutations* (London: Routledge and Kegan Paul, 1972), pp. 33–59.
[29] Joseph Wolpe and Stanley Rachman, 'Psychoanalytic "Evidence": A
Critique Based on Freud's Case of Little Hans', *The Journal of Nervous and
Mental Disease*, vol. cxxxi (1960), pp. 135–48.
[30] *Complete Psychological Works*, vol. xxii (1964), p. 80.

had written, in *The Ego and the Id*, 'Psychoanalysis is an
instrument to enable the ego to achieve a progressive conquest of the id.'[31]

Somewhere in this dream of culture, of progressive enlightenment, there lurks an impulse to intellectual suicide.
For Freud depended on that great mass of repressed matter,
the Unconscious, for the manipulable materials of his
scientific enterprise. It was as if every act of scientific illumination reduces the empire of the scientist, since each inert
piece of unconscious mechanism, once illuminated, is no
longer unconscious, no longer inert, no longer a mere mechanism. Science in rendering the Unconscious conscious
eliminates it. If this logic were correct, the effect of psychoanalysis, in the long run, would be to render psychoanalysis
itself no longer true, by removing that in human nature
which is susceptible of a quantifying analysis. Be that as it
may, the dream is a Stoic dream: reason is to triumph over
passion. Lawrence, on the other hand, is one of the greatest
anti-Stoic writers.

It would be unfair to leave this topic without adding a
rider. Anne Fernihough, in an admirable account of
Lawrence's clash with Freud, rightly points to Freud's sense
of triumphant intellectual conquest as something Lawrence
could not stomach. Freud certainly presents himself in this
way (we have already cited the phrase 'progressive conquest', from *The Ego and the Id*). But Anne Fernihough
draws on a different passage to support her case, Freud's
application to himself of the epithet 'conquistador'.[32] Freud
does indeed use this word in a letter he wrote to Wilhelm
Fliess on 1 February 1890, but the context, oddly enough, is
modest intellectually, the exact opposite of scientific pride:
'I am not really a man of science, not a thinker. I am nothing
but by temperament a Conquistador—an Adventurer if you

---

[31] *Complete Psychological Works*, vol. xix (1961), p. 56.
[32] *D. H. Lawrence: Aesthetics and Ideology* (Oxford: Oxford University
Press, 1993), p. 62.

want to translate the word—with the curiosity, the boldness and the tenacity that belongs to that kind of being.'[33] Of course a kind of pride asserts itself before the sentence is over, but it is not the pride of the lawgiver. The conquistador, as Freud imagines him, precedes the colonist—a wild man, willing to try anything, before the forces of reason and government appear. Here Freud half sees himself as we have come to see him; as a daring imagination. But such moments are exceedingly rare. Anne Fernihough's basic argument is entirely correct.

Earlier I compared Aristotle's notion of *catharsis* with Swift's antic farcical reduction of spirit to wind in *A Tale of a Tub*—but then set the comparison aside. Certainly Freud's famous derivation of religion from an original libidinal charge is strangely anticipated in Swift's *Mechanical Operation of the Spirit*:

The seed or principle which has ever put men upon *visions* in things *invisible*, is of a corporeal nature; for the profounder chemists inform us that the strongest *spirits* may be extracted from human flesh. Besides, the spinal marrow being nothing else but a continuation of the brain, must needs create a very free communication between the superior faculties and those below: and thus the *thorn in the flesh* serves for a *spur* to the *spirit*.[34]

When Swift writes '*thorn in the flesh*' he intends a sexual implication. This is made clear both by a reference a few lines earlier to the libertine practices of the Family of Love and by a further reference, a few lines after the passage quoted, to *furor uterinus* in female Quakers. *Furor uterinus* ('womb-rage') is glossed in the Oxford Authors *Jonathan Swift* as 'nymphomania'.[35] It is also, notice, a Latin translation of the Greek word which has come down to us as

[33] Quoted in Ernest Jones, *Sigmund Freud: Life and Work*, 3 vols. (London: Hogarth Press), 1956–7, vol. 1, p. 382.

[34] *Jonathan Swift*, The Oxford Authors, ed. Angus Ross and David Woolley (Oxford: Oxford University Press, 1980), p. 179.

[35] Ibid., p. 638.

hysteria: a term and a conception which was to haunt the thinking of Freud. Again we have to say that Swift is joking while Freud is not. But there is a charge of sheer intellectual energy in the passage from Swift which, so to speak, transcends the category 'joke'. Moreover, to look at Swift with his citations, half playful, half seriously learned, of heretical Gnostics and libertines like Simon Magus and the Family of Love, is to become aware that the structure of Freud's thought is not an innovation of the nineteenth century but, on the contrary, goes back a very long way. Epiphanius, a bishop of the fourth century, said that the Adamites (actually noted for asceticism) were really moved by lust.[36] Robert Burton in the seventeenth century gave a similar account of the Anabaptists of Münster.[37] The great difference between the older material and Freud is that the older accounts are all directed at heretical (that is supposedly depraved or distorted) religion. Think here of current attacks in the English newspapers on American TV evangelism with its continual stress on the intertwining of religious enthusiasm and sex. But Freud applied the notion to religion as a whole. In comparison with that difference, the worry about the degree to which Freud's theory is physicalist in its basic conception is of minor importance.

Freud also, through his conception of the unconscious, contrived a means of re-casting the very notion of wish-fulfilment which earlier seemed potentially fatal to Aristotle's theory of tragedy. It is as if Freud came up with a huge stratagem which is the reverse of the neo-Platonic one. Instead of putting the artist in touch with an ideal world, he links the artist to an underworld of *libido* and death-wish. Plotinus's term for the path taken by the artist includes a spatial prefix, *ana*, 'up': the artist *anatrechei*, 'up-runs',

[36] *Adversus Haereses*, 52, in *Epiphanii Episcopi Constantiae Opera*, ed. G. Dindorf, 5 vols. (Leipzig: T. O. Weigel, 1859), vol. ii, pp. 504–7.

[37] *Anatomie of Melancholy*, III. iii. 4. 2; ed. Thomas C. Faulkner, Nicholas K. Kiessling, and Rhonda L. Blair, 3 vols. (Oxford: Clarendon Press, 1989–94), vol. iii, p. 316.

'ascends' to the eternal Ideas. Freud's artist *katatrechei*, 'goes *down*' to the equally unchanging psychic underworld. Freud's artist must descend, like Orpheus, like Aeneas finding the way to his dead father, to the dark place under our feet. Indeed Freud thought that the analogy between poetry and investigative psychoanalysis was close. On the occasion of his seventieth birthday he expressly disclaimed the title 'discoverer of the Unconscious': 'The poets and philosophers before me discovered the Unconscious,' he said; 'What I discovered was the scientific method by which the Unconscious can be studied.'[38] The analyst too must first descend into the dark. As the epigraph on the title page of *The Interpretation of Dreams* Freud quotes a line from Virgil's *Aeneid*:

> *Flectere si nequeo superos, Acheronta movebo*
> If I cannot bend the will of the gods on high, I will stir up the river of hell.
>
> (*Aeneid*, vii. 312)

The Freudian ulterior realm seems better fitted than the Platonic to deal with the disturbing pleasure of tragedy.

Admittedly, in Freud's grand theory of art (as distinct from his more modest occasional observations on the subject) two elements jar. Freud believed that Shakespeare's *Hamlet* and Dostoevsky's *The Brothers Karamazov* owed their power entirely to the latent libidinal content, the slain father-rival, the erotic mother. What survives, perhaps from Freud's notoriously unpersuasive essay on Leonardo da Vinci,[39] is the intuition that *The Virgin and Child with St Anne and the Infant St John*, with its tumbling human figures gravely stilled in a composition of pyramidal stability, the visually bewildering composite female form issuing

[38] See Lionel Trilling, 'Freud and Literature', in his *The Liberal Imagination* (London: Mercury Books, 1961), p. 34.

[39] See Brian Farrell's introduction to the translation by Alan Tyson of Freud's *Leonardo da Vinci and a Memory of his Childhood* (Harmondsworth: Penguin Books, 1963).

at the top in two beautiful female heads, is the charged memory of a double mother (for Leonardo, as Freud points out, was passed to a foster mother). But Freud also wrote, in the *Introductory Lectures on Psychoanalysis*, that the difference between the artist and the neurotic fantasist is that the artist knows how to disguise his 'substitute gratifications' so effectively that they can be accepted and enjoyed by a large, heavily repressed public.[40] There is something odd here: communication of the libidinal makes the masterpiece; skill in disguising the libidinal makes the artist.

C. S. Lewis pressed hard on the first thesis when he objected to the sentence, 'Does it not begin to dawn upon us that many fairy tales which begin with the words "Once upon a time there were a king and queen" simply mean: "Once upon a time there were a father and mother".'[41] The crucial phrase is 'simply mean'—not 'mean *inter alia*' but 'mean this and nothing else', with the implication that the image, as distinct from the latent thought, effects nothing but disguise. Can it really be, Lewis asks, that we have been wholly deceived in thinking that the power of *Paradise Lost*, Book IV, when Satan gets into the Garden of Eden, lies in all those things of which we are conscious, the imagery, the subtle interplay of thought and action?[42] If this is true, then if we strip away the disguise and simply tell, directly, the sexual story—which will be about entering a female body— this new version should be at once much more powerful. But in fact many people obstinately find the Miltonic story *more* exciting than the bare, libidinal 'story'.

[40] *Complete Psychological Works*, vol. xvi (1963), p. 376.
[41] 'Psychoanalysis and Literary Criticism', in *They Asked for a Paper* (London: Geoffrey Bles, 1962), pp. 120–38, esp. pp. 127–32. Lewis is quoting from the translation of *The Introductory Lectures on Psychoanalysis* by Joan Rivière (London: George Allen and Unwin, 2nd edn., 1933), p. 134. The translation given in the *Complete Psychological Works*, vol. xvi (1963), p. 159, gives 'only mean to say' in place of 'simply mean'.
[42] In his *Preface to Paradise Lost* (London: Oxford University Press, 1960), p.49, Lewis says that the adjective 'hairy', applied by Milton to the garden's vegetable wall at IV. 135, looks Freudian.

Lewis knew about the second thesis of psychoanalysis in which the mechanisms of repression are emphasized. We are not only libidinal beings, we are also comprehensively repressed beings (indeed, if we were not repressed, there would be no such thing as the Unconscious). Therefore we are *not allowed* to enjoy the libidinal material directly; all sorts of alarm bells are jangling, the mind's police are being mobilized. It is at this point that Lewis becomes clever. 'Fine,' he says, in effect, 'I understand that.' But if we're not allowed to enjoy the libidinal material directly and are obliged to get our pleasure indirectly by way of muffling images, what is one to make of the medieval poem, Guillaume de Lorris's *Le Roman de la Rose*? In this poem the plucking of the rose means exactly what Freud would have it mean, but the poet has sign-posted everything, made this meaning explicitly clear. The imagery, therefore, cannot be there to provide an essential disguise. It really looks very much as if the poet and his audience were interested in *both* sex *and* gardens—and in the rich imaginative commerce between the two.

The argument hits hard. I remember a Freudian saying, in response to Lewis's essay, 'Well, by the time of Guillaume de Lorris *some* interest has, as it were, rubbed off on to roses from their libidinal application in the previous poems.' But when was that? Guillaume de Lorris died in 1237, more than a hundred and sixty years before the death of Chaucer. Lewis has in effect relegated a supposedly universal theory of art to a remote period. I once heard a lecturer maintain the fierce primary thesis that *Hamlet* owes its status as a literary masterpiece to the hidden libidinal matter. At question time I asked, 'What about the earlier play of *Hamlet*, perhaps by Kyd?' This probably contained roughly the same libidinal understory. Did the lecturer really think that if this text had survived, it would have been ranked above, say, *Antony and Cleopatra*? I sat down, thinking that I had won. The lecturer replied, 'Yes, it would.' It would seem that a

recipe for producing world masterpieces is now available—
for anyone can tuck an Oedipal story behind enough images
to keep the conscience quiet.

The duality in Freud's thought means that traditional
literary analysis, at first set aside as concerned with shadows
not substance, can come back into play. On the one hand we
have the Ego (committed to all the restrictions imposed by
the Reality Principle) and on the other the Id (in which the
Pleasure Principle reigns unchecked). The reader may now
be affected at two levels: the Ego is pleased by its proper
nourishment, the Id by its. Certain puzzling features remain;
for example, the strange clairvoyance by which the Id suc-
ceeds in picking up information effectively screened from
the Ego (usually the Ego is regarded as intellectually the
sharper of the two!). Freud once observed, a little helplessly,
that it is a very remarkable thing that the Unconscious of
one human being can react upon another, without passing
through the Conscious.[43] He adds, hopefully, that the phenomenon 'deserves closer investigation'. Meanwhile, however,
if the Ego hates what the Id loves, the Ego really has certain
loves, certain pleasures *of its own.*

Readers of Freud's *Civilization and its Discontents* do not
always notice how the celebrated opposition between the
Reality Principle and the Pleasure Principle evaporates in
that book. Freud said that European humanity was sexually
maimed, that the blood-red primal gratification of original
desire was curbed by the deadening restrictions of civilization. But when he explains how this happened, the logic is
that of descriptive Utilitarianism. Freud's State of Nature is
more like the fierce 'war of every man against every man' in
Hobbes's *Leviathan*[44] than it is like the polite Arcadia of
Locke's *Second Treatise on Government. Lupus est homo*

---

[43] In his essay on 'The Unconscious', *Complete Psychological Works*, vol.
xiv (1957), p. 194.

[44] *Leviathan* I. xiii; ed. Richard Tuck (Cambridge: Cambridge University
Press, 1991), p. 88.

homini, 'Man is a wolf to man'.[45] In this primal time libidinal joy expressed itself in physical cruelty. Therefore for every gratified strong libidinal agent there would be a larger number of bleeding victims (experiencing not masochistic pleasure but straight pain). The weak multitude then discover that they can avoid pain by imposing collectively enforced sanctions on strong individuals. We are now in the Utilitarian world of the Hedonic Calculus, the calculation of pleasure against pain. For this calculation to work, pleasure and pain must form parts of a single system of currency. At first indeed, Freud's picture looks like a version of *Paradise Lost.* Never again such joy. But the multitude would not have combined as they did had they not believed that the elimination of pain was fairly purchased by the virtual extinction of such pleasure. A hedonic calculus cannot operate to produce an overall *reduction* of happiness. Statistically, across the board, as politicians say, the movement must represent an advance; less joy, indeed, but therewith *much* less pain.

Yet, when all this is said, one senses that someone like Nietzsche would resist—would wish to say that the black and scarlet of the original state is infinitely better than the later greyness—and you can forget your Utilitarian calculus. And part of Freud's mind would eagerly assent. The psychoanalytic art critic Ernst Kris was willing to cross the floor and locate the pleasure of art in the Ego: 'The shifts in cathexis of mental energy which the work of art elicits or facilitates are, we believe, pleasurable in themselves.'[46] Norman Holland made the same fundamental move when he wrote his psychoanalytic account of Matthew Arnold's 'Dover Beach'. We find the poem beautiful and powerful, he argued, because it offers a defensive adaptation—a formal management—of an anxiety-laden fantasy. He presented a substantially parallel reading of Macbeth's soliloquy on the vanity of

---

[45] Plautus, *Asinaria,* 495.
[46] *Psychoanalytic Explorations in Art* (New York: International University Press, 1952), p. 16.

life. 'In pleasing,' he wrote, 'the crucial elements lie more at the defensive than at the fantasy level.'[47] It is clear that we are moving rapidly backwards, in the direction of the old formalist theory, 'Tragedy pleases because of the formal control it provides.' This is to exploit the light side—one might almost say, the familiar element in Freud's scheme. But the dark side of the theory—the side which says there is that in us which actively *desires* death and violence—seems obstinately to offer more to one baffled by the pleasure of tragedy.

After all, by this doctrine nightmare can easily be re-interpreted as wish-fulfilment. The dream of a parent's death, with all its attendant grief, may represent a wish at the level of the Unconscious. I said, at the very beginning of this book, that if we were all wicked there would be no puzzle in our joy at the pain or death of the protagonist. I said that with an easy assumption that it was self-evident that few are wicked in that way. But Freud's work purported to reveal subterranean places, cellars of the mind in all of us where wishes wholly unacceptable to the Super-Ego rage continually. Does this indicate the direction in which our thoughts should now move? In other words, is Aristotle unable to proceed because, paradoxically enough, he is too much confined to the brightly illuminated area of reason? Freud makes virtually no use of Aristotle, but his thought was nourished from the beginning by Greek myths. Could the myths—the tigers of wrath—be wiser than the horses of instruction?[48] Aristotle's thought is Apollonian, but the theatre in which *Oedipus Rex* was performed was dedicated to a deity of another stamp, Dionysus, the god of the irra-tional. Earlier in this lecture I resisted Nietzschean language; now I begin to loosen the restriction. To explore this ques-

[47] *The Dynamics of Literary Response* (New York and London: Oxford University Press, 1968), p. 224.
[48] William Blake, 'The Proverbs of Hell', *The Marriage of Heaven and Hell*, in *The Poems of William Blake*, ed. D. V. Erdman and W. H. Stevenson (London: Longman, 1972), p. 110.

tion is to involve oneself in an immense inversion of what is still the commonest view of classical antiquity—that is to say, a picture of the ancient world as a place of reason and light. This darkening of antiquity will be the principal matter of the next chapter.

3

THE GAME OF DEATH

My last chapter ended with Freud and with the question, 'Does the admission of a dark side of the mind—an unconscious—have a bearing on the problem of the pleasure of tragedy?'

Behind this darkening of the mind, however, there lies another darkening, of our picture of the ancient sources of European literature. Antiquity, formerly given over to the Ego, becomes itself the province of the Id. Roughly speaking, a sunlit, rational, enlightened world, peopled as it were by marble figures in a state of tranquil felicity (think of Winckelmann) was replaced, retrospectively, by an opposite world: blood guilt and sacrifice, dream and vision, orgiastic music, unreason. One way of expressing this change is to say that the pretence of Augustanism was dropped: instead of assuming that antiquity was somehow full of eighteenth-century rationalists having either no religion or a religion etiolated and simplified to the point of minimal Deism, it was at last noticed that the ancient world pullulates with spirits and deities, is crammed with unreasonable, alarming powers. This, by the way, is simply true.

Within this general darkening we find a particular thesis about Greek drama—namely, that Greek tragedy was fundamentally ritual, that it was religious in ways which moderns find difficult. There is an entry in one of Leonardo da Vinci's notebooks which reads, 'The sun has never seen any shadow.'[1] Leonardo is here thinking like a good Albertian

[1] W ('Windsor') 12669 *recto* (MSS catalogued by Kenneth Clark, Cambridge, 1935); in *Selections from the Notebooks of Leonardo da Vinci*, ed. Irma A. Richter (London: Oxford University Press, 1952), p. 54.

perspectival painter; it has suddenly struck him that for an
eye which is itself the source of light, shadows will always be
on the far side of any object. For such an eye darkness is
essentially and systematically suppressed. For the Greek the
sun was Apollo (called 'most powerful eye' in Sophocles'
Trachiniae, 101). But Apollo, god of unshadowed light, was
not the only deity in the pantheon. There was also, for
example, Dionysus, the god not only of intoxication but also
of wildness, green nature, of the irrational. One way to
represent the change of which I am speaking might be to
say, 'Apollo had been honoured for centuries; now Dionysus
was given his due.' And of course this antithesis is Nietzschean.

The effects of the transformation are all around us in
modernist writing. Joyce's *Ulysses* is not just a twentieth-
century mock-heroic; Joyce used the *Odyssey* as a quarry,
not of rational certainties to be subverted, but for magic
and metamorphosis. Eliot in *The Waste Land* deployed a
Frazerian intuition: ancient European history and blood
sacrifice linked to fertility. The movement appears in different forms in many places. Jane Harrison's *Themis* and
Gilbert Murray's writings on the Dionysiac Year Spirit, as
we shall see, belong in this line.

Nor was Nietzsche the first to notice the murky side of
the ancient world. Earlier rationalists were sometimes either
too learned or too sharp to preserve the inherited blindness.
Frazer's *The Golden Bough* itself is in some ways a nine-
teenth-century rationalist work, finding the courage to be
critical of antiquity for its very failures in enlightenment.
Time and time again, Frazer can sound like Gibbon[2]—for
example in his account of 'Saint Hippolytus'[3] or when he

---

[2] Robert Ackerman says that Frazer's style is a mixture of Addison and
Gibbon, the Gibbonian element prevailing 'when he seeks to soar or impress',
in his *J. G. Frazer: His Life and Work* (Cambridge: Cambridge University
Press, 1987), p. 23. See also J. G. Frazer, 'Gibbon at Lausanne', in his *Creation
and Evolution in Primitive Cosmogonies and Other Pieces* (London:
Macmillan, 1935), pp. 47–52.

says that 'the good taste and humanity of the Greeks must have recoiled from the more violent rites of the Magna Mater'.[4] In the pages immediately following, Frazer explains how introversion, stemming from the East, corrupted the ideal of public service, until the Renaissance brought back 'saner, manlier views of the world'.[5] It will be said that the word 'manly' is richly Victorian, but in fact Gibbon speaks of 'the manly pride of the Romans'.[6] Mistrust of the Near East reappears, of course, in Nietzsche. There is a certain affinity between *The Golden Bough* and, say, the Pitt-Rivers Museum in Oxford, with its vast array of blood-curdling fetishes, among which Christian votive offerings—by design —fail to stand out as different. *Tantum religio potuit suadere malorum*, 'So much evil could religion do.'[7] Hume likewise, in his *Natural History of Religion*, written before 1757—130 years before Nietzsche's *Genealogy of Morals*— though not published until 1777, saw religion in naturalist, evolutionary terms rather than as a structure of revealed, unchanging verities. Hume has no doubt about the irrational character of ancient religion. I suppose we smell Modern- ism, not when antiquity is shown to be irrational, but when the irrationality is itself gratefully embraced.

Eliot would resist, but I feel this is palpably true of *The Waste Land*. There is a considerable irony in Eliot's growing up in a time of world-weary scepticism and then finding something like religious belief only when he turned to a book designed to show the absurdity or wickedness of ritu- ally based religion.[8] Eliot disregarded the instructions on

[3] *The Golden Bough: A Study in Magic and Religion*, Part I, *The Magic Art*, 2 vols. (London: Macmillan, 1921), vol. i, p. 21.
[4] Ibid., Part IV, *Adonis, Attis, Osiris*, 2 vols. (London: Macmillan, 1914), vol. i, p. 299.   [5] Ibid., p. 301.
[6] *The History of the Decline and Fall of the Roman Empire*, ed. J. B. Bury, 7 vols. (London: Methuen, 1909–14), vol. xi, p. 169.
[7] Lucretius, *De Rerum Natura*, I. 101.
[8] Frazer says that he reveres the moral and philosophical core of Christi- anity, but regards the ritual aspects as an accommodation to baser needs: *Adonis, Attis, Osiris*, vol. i, p. 311.

the bottle. Milton in his *Nativity Ode* had, back in the seventeenth century, beaten Frazer to some of his material (Milton's 'wounded Thammuz'[9] is Frazer's Adonis), but for Milton, unlike Eliot, these sanguinary deities were enemies of true religion, to be hunted from their lairs at the birth of Christ. For Eliot it is rather as if all the voices are somehow telling one thing, resurrection, life out of death. The Eliot of *The Waste Land* is not yet Christian, but I think one can smell it coming. I am suggesting, I suppose, that Eliot's talk of tradition is in fact the masking of an almost solipsistic terror, and that his Christianity (which I take to be real and strong) was something reached in darkness by a route other than that of reason. He loved Dante but his thought (though never exactly Nietzschean) is much less close to Aquinas than it is to Schopenhauer—the first major European philosopher after Plato to turn to Indian religion. Schopenhauer had a bust of Buddha in his room and kept a poodle called Atma ('World-soul'). The Jesuit philosopher Coplestone has noticed, incidentally, that Bergson, whose influence on Eliot is undoubted, is himself remarkably like Schopenhauer.[10] It may seem that my references are multiplying unmanageably. I am saying, in a way, that Eliot, unable to find a reason for his faith, found an un-reason for it. Again, the cadence is Nietzschean: 'Man would sooner will the Nothing, than not will at all.'[11] Nietzsche, indeed, is a theological nihilist and Eliot is not. Eliot's God, like Nietzsche's, died, but then, unlike Nietzsche's, rose again.

Incidentally, Frazer did not fail to notice the analogy between Christian and pagan materials:

[9] 'Nativity Ode', 101. Cf. *Paradise Lost*, I. 452–3, 'Of Thammuz yearly wounded: the love-tale / Infected Sion's daughters'.

[10] F. Coplestone, *A History of Philosophy*, 7 vols. (New York: Doubleday), vol. vii, Part II (1963), p. 36.

[11] 'Lieber will noch der Mensch das Nichts wollen als nicht wollen', the last sentence of *The Genealogy of Morals* (my translation); in *Nietzsches Werke*, ed. G. Colli, M. Montinari *et al.*, 8 vols. (Berlin: Walter de Gruyter), vol. vi. 2 (1982), p. 430.

. . . it appears from the testimony of an anonymous Christian, who wrote in the fourth century of our era, that Christian and pagans alike were struck by the remarkable coincidence between the death and resurrection of their respective deities, and that the coincidence formed the theme of bitter controversy between the adherents of the rival religions, the pagans contending that the resurrection of Christ was a spurious imitation of the resurrection of Attis, and the Christians asserting with equal warmth that the resurrection of Attis was a diabolical counterfeit of the resurrection of Christ. In these unseemly bickerings the heathen took what to a superficial observer might seem strong ground by arguing that their god was the older and therefore presumably the original, not the counterfeit, since as a general rule an original is older than its copy. This feeble argument the Christians easily rebutted. They admitted, indeed, that in point of time Christ was the junior deity, but they triumphantly demonstrated his real seniority by falling back on the subtlety of Satan, who on so important an occasion had surpassed himself by inverting the usual order of nature.[12]

Frazer's chosen stylistic posture is again one of Gibbonian contempt for all concerned—but especially for the Christians. Eliot conversely is like one of the benighted contestants (remember Eliot's defence of those who in the Middle Ages read Virgil's Fourth Eclogue as a prophecy of Christ's coming).[13] If the Enlightenment had bleached the ancient world then Nietzsche, more than anyone else, was the agent of its darkening. Yet Nietzsche's own relation to the Enlightenment is more intimate than is commonly realized. His assault on Christianity preserves many features of the previous Enlightenment assault. The general picture here is

---

[12] *The Golden Bough*, Part iv, *Adonis, Attis, Osiris*, vol. i, pp. 309–10. Frazer wrote in a letter to George Macmillan (8 November 1889): 'The resemblance of many of the savage customs and ideas to the fundamental doctrines of Christianity is striking. But I make no reference to this parallelism, leaving my readers to draw their own conclusions, one way or the other' (quoted in Robert Ackerman, *J. G. Frazer: His Life and Work*, p. 95). In fact, as we see, Frazer *did* refer to the parallelism.

[13] *On Poetry and Poets* (London: Faber and Faber, 1957), pp. 121–3.

indeed of a sunlit, healthful ancient society succeeded by a set of weak, envious, down-trodden persons, followers of a Slave Ethic which glorified torture and humiliation. This picture can be found in Gibbon who, as he tells us in his famous *Memoir*, was first moved to write his great history by the sight of the bare-footed friars going to sing vespers in (what had been) the temple of Jupiter Capitoline. There, as he watched in the evening September sunshine (so his account runs), a gust of indignation ran through him and the idea 'started into' his mind. He would tell the story of the 'decline and fall of the Roman Empire'[14] and 'the triumph of barbarism and religion'.[15] A foul priest-ridden religion of slaves, meeting furtively, displaced the noble civilization of the Antonines. Gibbon even says that the Christians, finding their poverty inescapable, *claimed it as a virtue*.[16] This passage immediately follows a quotation from Tertullian's *De Spectaculis*—the very same paragraph which Nietzsche quotes at a parallel moment in *The Genealogy of Morals*.[17]

Notice that Gibbon, like all great historians, is addressing a puzzle: how did the weak defeat the strong? How did this terrible thing happen? This is likewise the grand puzzle of *The Genealogy of Morals*. Roughly speaking, the answer there is that the noble blond beast—I have borrowed the blond beast from *Twilight of the Idols*, but he will serve here—may be imagined strolling along, swinging his club—and then falling abruptly into a spiked pit, dug overnight by the runtish slave-men, working away with little spades, co-operating in their *ressentiment* of strength and beauty. The noble is unreflective and they are cunning (one is tempted

[14] *The Memoirs of the Life of J. Edward Gibbon*, ed. G. Birkbeck Hill (London: Methuen, 1900), p. 167.
[15] *Decline and Fall of the Roman Empire*, vol. vii, p. 321.
[16] Ibid., vol. ii, p. 38. Cf. ibid., p. 70, '. . . dregs of the populace, of peasants and mechanics, of dogs and women, of beggars and slaves'.
[17] *The Birth of Tragedy and The Genealogy of Morals*, trans. Francis Golffing (New York: Doubleday, 1956), p. 183.

to say, 'intelligent'). It is of course a picture of the rise of Christianity which has taken quite a beating recently. Robin Lane Fox has shown that early Christianity was really a very middle-class affair.[18]

Nietzsche dedicated *Human, All Too Human*—admittedly in one of his spasmodic reactions against Schopenhauer[19]—to Voltaire, saint of the Enlightenment. The connection between the two is, moreover, corroborated by a minor miracle. On 30 May 1878, Nietzsche received through the post a bust of Voltaire with a slip of paper which read, 'L'âme de Voltaire fait ses compliments à Frédéric Nietzsche.'[20]

The myth of decline into Christianity is an Enlightenment myth. Nietzsche's kind of antisemitism (indeed less violent than that of many of his contemporaries) has affinities with Enlightenment antisemitism, in that it is cultural rather than racial. Virginia Woolf's father Leslie Stephen once observed that the high priests of eighteenth-century toleration are united in their hostility to the Jews.[21] The twentieth century is shocked by this, but there is a rationale, of sorts. They are against the Jews because they believe the Jews themselves to be enemies of toleration—the source of priestcraft, spiritual tyranny, the frightening of children through guilt, and so on—all these things are seen as Hebraic, as counter-Hellenic. It is almost as if, after centuries of

[18] *Pagans and Christians* (Harmondsworth: Penguin Books, 1986), pp. 293–312, 319–20.

[19] See M. S. Silk and J. P. Stern, *Nietzsche and Tragedy* (Cambridge: Cambridge University Press, 1981), p. 114.

[20] See W. D. Williams, *Nietzsche and the French: A Study of the Influence of Nietzsche's French Reading on his Thought and Writing* (Oxford: Blackwell, 1952), p. 52. Frau F. Nietzsche later wondered whether the whole affair was a joke engineered by one Gersdorff, a boyhood friend. See *Selected Letters of Nietzsche*, trans. A. M. Ludovici (London: Soho Book Co., 1985), p. 116.

[21] *History of English Thought in the Eighteenth Century*, 2 vols. (London: Hart-Davis, 1962), vol. i, p. 141.

being hated as the murderers of Christ, the Jews were now to be hated as the source of Christianity.

Nietzsche's celebrated evolutionary account of ethics in *The Genealogy of Morals* is as much an outgrowth from Enlightenment historiography as it is a subversion of it. Indeed, it is interesting to ask, how *ethically* revolutionary is *The Genealogy of Morals?* When Nietzsche attacks Christianity on the ground that it is fuelled by hatred and envy, his thought is, it seems to me, *ethically* entirely conventional. As an account of Christianity it is indeed both disturbing and disruptive—that is quite another matter. He is saying, 'Christianity is not—has not been in fact—what it pretends to be. Christians prate of love but really they are driven by hate.' But notice how such passages can be read by Christians in a penitential spirit of grateful assent. The reason is simple: Nietzsche here presupposes that love is good and hatred bad. Were this not the case, his words would not constitute an attack. On other occasions Nietzsche really is *ethically subversive.* Such passages are instantly detectable because they cause the gorge to rise, in a quite different way.

For example:

Not so very long ago a royal wedding or a great public celebration would have been incomplete without executions, tortures and *autos da fé*, a noble household without some person whose office it was to serve as a butt for everyone's malice or cruel teasing . . . To behold suffering gives pleasure, but to cause another to suffer affords an even greater pleasure![22]

The surrounding prose is rather slippery but, quite inescapably, Nietzsche is commending this cruelty. At such points his attack on altruism becomes *ethically* fundamental. There is a shift from 'Apparently altruistic behaviour is commonly self-seeking' (which continues to privilege real altruism as a virtue) to 'Altruism, pity, etc. are themselves contemptible, forms of weakness, a lowering of health' (the notorious attack on pity at *Antichrist*, 1. 7, is of this kind).[23] Yet even in these shocking passages, the Enlightenment myth of descent is discernibly still operative. Given that Nietzsche has chosen, as his set project, to give an account of the genetics of morality, we might have expected a work in which all morality would be explained away—shown to be historically determined by extra-ethical factors, to be a mere fluctuating epiphenomenon upon the struggle for life—or some such. But the story which Nietzsche tells—in which terms for 'good' begin as the self-description of the strong, noble people—is presented by him as a sort of 'Fall-narrative': an original ethical truth distorted by introversion. In a manner deeply congenial to the eighteenth century he is in effect using 'nature' as a source of *pre*scription: 'This is what we *are*, basically, originally; therefore [logical leap] this is the way we *ought* to be; the first truth is the real truth, the rest lies.' Nietzsche, it would seem, is profoundly the opposite of Aristotle. Aristotle as a working biologist tends to see things as most fully themselves when they reach the end of a complex development. Nietzsche, conversely, tends to be an eager victim of 'the Genetic Fallacy' ('Oak trees are disguised acorns'). It is one of many characteristics which he shares with Freud; Freud once wrote to his fiancée, 'What we once were . . . [we] in part still remain.'[24]

The Genealogy of Morals (1887) is Gibbonian in so far as it finds health and sunlit splendour in the ancient world, and introversion, priestcraft, asceticism, and torture in the post-classical. Thus far, one might say, Hellas is still bright, is as yet undarkened. Even in the *Genealogy*, however, we can also find a marked hostility to the objectivist element in Greek philosophy and this hostility Gibbon could not

[23] *The Complete Works of Friedrich Nietzsche*, ed. Oscar Levy, 18 vols. (Edinburgh and London: T. N. Fontis, 1909–13), vol. xvi (1911), pp. 131–2.
[24] See Ernest Jones, *Sigmund Freud: Life and Work*, 3 vols. (London: Hogarth Press, 1953–7), vol. i, p. 191.

endorse. 'Let us, from now on,' Nietzsche writes, 'be on our guard against the hallowed philosopher's myth of a pure, will-less, painless, timeless knower . . . All seeing is essentially perspective, and so is all knowing.'[25] It will be said that Nietzsche is here thinking of Kant, but he must have known that these are ideas having their roots in Plato and Aristotle. There is in fact a curious reticence in the *Genealogy* with regard to ancient philosophy. He is happy to talk of warriors, kings, gods, and poets, but the thinkers are, one senses, an embarrassment. Therefore, from an Enlightenment point of view, even in the *Genealogy* one of the lamps —perhaps the most important one, the lamp of reason— has been turned off.

In the earlier *Birth of Tragedy* (1870–1) this darkening of antiquity is explicit. The Socratic spirit was fatal, says Nietzsche, to tragedy: the hated Euripides is the poet of 'aesthetic Socratism'.[26] Moreover, tragedy itself, a high point of culture for Nietzsche, is seen not as *Aufklärung* but rather as a *chiaroscuro*, the bright god, Apollo, in tension with the dark god, Dionysus. In consequence Sophocles' Oedipus loses his marmoreal quality and assumes the lineaments— one can almost say—of Kurtz in Conrad's *Heart of Darkness*:

It is as if, though the myth whispered to us that wisdom, and especially Dionysiac wisdom, is an unnatural crime, and that whoever in pride of knowledge hurls nature into the abyss of destruction must himself experience nature's disintegration.[27]

Set against that passage from Nietzsche this from Conrad:

. . . he had stepped over edge, while I had been permitted to draw back my hesitating foot . . . perhaps all the wisdom, and all truth, and all sincerity, are just compressed into that inappreciable moment of time in which we step over the threshold of the invis-

[25] *The Genealogy of Morals*, p. 255.
[26] *The Birth of Tragedy*, pp. 77–82.
[27] Ibid., p. 61.

ible . . . it was an affirmation, a moral victory paid for by in-
numerable defeats, by abominable terrors, by abominable satis-
factions.[28]

The ancient association of knowledge with light is here
being prised apart. The *deepest* knowledge is now fused
with a formless darkness. The effects of this prising apart
upon modern literature are incalculable.

We have reached a point of profound subversion. Yet
here also Nietzsche's thought proved to be not only progressive but also violently retrogressive. Plato is not just an
inadvertent (retrospectively selected) enemy. Plato himself
fought against the doctrines of Heraclitus and Cratylus,
philosophers of flux and disintegration. Nietzsche contrari-
wise (with a little help from Schopenhauer) is fighting *for*
flux and disintegration, against Kant, whom he sees as ab-
solutist. It is worth remembering how Plato opposed Pro-
tagorean perspectivalism (see his critique of 'man the
measure of all things' in the *Theaetetus*, 160C–171D). The
speech given to Callicles (despised by Plato) in the *Gorgias*
(492) can be read as a pre-emptive satire on *The Genealogy
of Morals*. Callicles says,

How can a man be happy who is the servant of anything? . . . He
who would truly live ought to allow his desires to wax to the
uttermost, and not to chastise them . . . he should have the courage
. . . to satisfy all his longings. And this I affirm to be natural justice
and nobility.

Think also of Thrasymachus in Book I of *The Republic*.

There is one element in the scheme of *The Birth of
Tragedy* which is endlessly misreported in undergraduate
essays and also in published writings. Dionysus, they say, is
the god of the dream world. Nietzsche himself says the exact
opposite: Apollo is the god of dream.[29] Nietzsche *contrasts*

---

[28] (London: J. M. Dent, 1946), p. 151.
[29] *The Birth of Tragedy*, pp. 19–20.

dream with Dionysiac intoxication. All the rest is as we expect: Apollo is the god of 'plastic powers'—of form—and of light, while Dionysus is associated with music, which is the expression of Schopenhauerian Will,[30] in all its murky, pre-rational freedom (you will recall that Schopenhauer works with two principles—*idea*, a formalizing agent and *will*, which is a sort of existential darkness). I suspect that the tendency of undergraduates to align Dionysus with dream, against the instructions of the author, has something to do with Sigmund Freud, for in Freud the dream-world, though subject to modification, gives us some sense of the anarchic powers of the Unconscious.

You will realize that now, having striven to show an affinity between Nietzsche and the eighteenth-century Enlightenment, I am now making it my business to show that he is nevertheless more subversive than Freud, who in *Civilisation and its Discontents* was more than half-willing to see the pleasure principle domesticated by a species of Utilitarian calculus. Similarly it is Nietzsche who is more powerfully linked to the disintegrative impulse of modernism. Freud believes in the reality of the world investigated by science. Nietzsche, in this a true disciple of Schopenhauer, does not. The god of light is for him a god of unreality—of 'fair illusion'.[31] He equivocates, as many have done before and since, on the Greek word '*phainomena*', 'appearances'; for the empirical scientist reality is made of phenomena but, meanwhile, 'appearance' in ordinary usage is naturally opposed to reality. Thus Nietzsche contrasts the core of things with 'the phenomenal world'.[32] Similarly he later uses the Kantian phrase '*Ding an sich*', 'thing-in-itself', to privilege music above 'phenomenon'.[33] Once again we must add that Schopenhauer stands between Kant and Nietzsche. Schopen-

[30] See 'The Metaphysics of Music', *The World as Will and Idea*, trans. R. B. Haldane and J. Kemp (London: Kegan Paul, Trench and Tubner, 1896), vol. iii, p. 232.

[31] *The Birth of Tragedy*, p. 22.　　　　　　　　　[32] Ibid., p. 53.

[33] Ibid., p. 99.

hauer identified the mysterious ulterior reality of the Kantian 'thing-in-itself' first with pure will and then, as we have
seen, with music.[34]

One reason why Nietzsche cannot adopt the usual charac-
terization of Apollo as god of knowledge is that, for him,
Apollo is associated with the principle of individuation,
itself a source of illusions. Most of us, unsubdued by
Schopenhauer, tend to assume that the apprehension of
finite existents might give knowledge, but all this is rejected
by Nietzsche. The rejection comes very close to generating
the weird conclusion, 'Existents don't exist; Unbeing alone
Is.' The notion of a potent Nothingness which by a converse
energy becomes ontologically stronger than mere things is
of course endemic in post-Nietzschean Existentialism—
especially in the (now despised) Sartre. Indeed the history
of Structuralism and Deconstruction may be understood
along these lines. Lévi-Strauss as a proto-structuralist
admittedly discarded as unusable the *néant* of Sartrean
philosophical psychology and chose as his material the
constituted self which appears in discourse.[35] But he never
loses the sense that such public realities are in some way a
series of fictions. Postmodernist Deconstruction, conversely
but predictably, re-asserts the *néant* by demonstrating the
infinitely recessive character of purportedly rational discourse. Schopenhauer, so to speak, saw all this coming.
He is careful to explain how he has a sense for the word
'nothing' which is ontologically positive.[36] He writes, 'We
have recognized the inmost nature of the world as will,
and all its phenomena as only the objectivity of will . . . with
the free denial, the surrender of will, all these phenomena
are also abolished . . . Before us there is certainly only

[34] *The World as Will and Idea*, vol. iii, p. 232.
[35] See *The Savage Mind* (London: Weidenfeld and Nicolson, 1972),
pp. 246–7 and Sartre, *Critique de la raison dialectique* (Paris: Gallimard,
1960), p. 183.
[36] *The World as Will and Idea*, vol. i, p. 528, vol. iii, p. 272.

nothingness.'[37] Hence the bizarre, irresponsible gaiety, founded upon nihilism, which characterizes Nietzsche.

On the one hand we have Nietzsche and his *epigoni*, Cornford, Jane Harrison, Gilbert Murray, E. R. Dodds, and A. W. H. Adkins telling us *as a matter of scholarship* that the ancient world in general and ancient tragedy in particular was permeated by religion, and on the other hand we have Aristotle. The prime peculiarity for twentieth-century readers (though not for any previous century) is this: Aristotle, who was there, appears not to know that Greek tragedy was religious.

In a curious uncritical fashion we carry in our heads two perhaps incompatible pictures of our own century: first, that we are the first people to perceive the intractably fluid character of all reality, and secondly that we are the first genuinely to understand the past, as something firmly distinct from ourselves. Some readers of *The Genealogy of Morals* assume, without discomfort, that the demonstration of the perspectival character of all knowledge is there *founded*—properly and objectively(!) in a great corrective movement of Scholarship: Gibbon's Romans are eighteenth-century gentlemen transposed; Tennyson's medievals are Victorians at heart, but Nietzsche's Greeks are Greeks. It is possible, I would suggest, that on the contrary, the scholarship is infected by the prior espousal of an inversely religious anti-rationalism. Cultural projection is insidious. It can insinuate itself into the most strenuous asseveration of objectivity, it can lurk in the most modest disclaimer. What if it should prove that even the gallant attempt to acknowledge the proper foreign-ness of ancient culture were really, at bottom, just an up-dated wish-projection? What if the dislodging of the Victorian Greeks of Verrall and Jebb were swiftly followed by a picture of Greek culture which is not pre-Romantic, but rather full of the willed primitivism of the post-Romantic? The eighteenth century, with good reason, thought itself a critical age. Today it is almost embarrassingly evident where that claim holds and where it fails. What if it were the special prerogative of the twentieth-century critic to transform the troglodytic master of Altamira into Picasso?

What, then, of the ritual character of Greek tragedy? What was the ritual? Once again the main line of the modern answer seems to stem from Nietzsche. He says in *The Birth of Tragedy* that the real ritual subject of Greek tragedy is the sufferings of Dionysus; he anchors this by alleging that for a long period the dramas actually dealt with this explicitly as their principal subject.[38]

There is no evidence whatever for this assertion. Moreover the consequences of the theory are, so to speak, internally peculiar. For example, Gilbert Murray found himself arguing that Pentheus in the *Bacchae*, the priggish, would-be oppressor of Dionysiac worship, 'is only another form of Dionysus himself'. You will recall that this person who punishes and destroys Pentheus in this play is—Dionysus.

On 3 January 1889, Nietzsche collapsed in the Piazza San Carlo, Turin, insane. In the following days he sent off a series of letters to friends, signed either 'The Crucified' or 'Dionysos'.[39] The real structure of Nietzsche's projected myth of Greek tragedy is almost embarrassingly evident. The last two sentences of the autobiographical *Ecce Homo* read, 'Have I been understood? Dionysos against the Crucified.'[40] To adopt the words of another prophet of the modern European mind, Albert Camus, Nietzsche finds the

---

[38] *The Birth of Tragedy*, pp. 57, 65–6.
[39] See Michael Tanner, 'Dim Perceptions of Clear Ones', *Times Literary Supplement*, 12–18 May 1989, p. 509.
[40] *Werke*, ed. G. Colli and M. Montinari, vol. vi. 3 (1969), p. 372.

only Christ we deserve.[41] Nietzsche, whose god, you will recall, died, needed a special resurrection; he needed, so to speak, a Christ with an altered physiognomy:

> And what rough beast, its hour come round at last,
> Slouches towards Bethlehem to be born?[42]

From Nietzsche the torch passed to Gilbert Murray. Murray presents the central myth as the story of the *Eniautos Daimon*, or Year Spirit. The cardinal points of the myth are as follows:

1. *Agon* (Summer versus Winter).
2. *Pathos* of the Year Daimon—ritual or sacrificial death.
3. Messenger announces the *pathos*.
4. *Threnos*—clash of contrary emotions, the death of the old being also the triumph of the new.
5. *Anagnorisis* of the Slain Daimon.
6. Epiphany and Theophany-in-glory of the Slain Daimon.[43]

Murray seems to have derived these features of the archetypal ritual principally from a study of the extant, ectypal plays. So it is not really surprising that the whole picture is rather suggestive of a Greek tragedy. What *is* surprising (in the circumstances) is that no extant play contains an epiphany of the protagonist, as Pickard-Cambridge pointed out in his complete (though largely ignored) demolition of Murray's theory.[44] Pickard-Cambridge allows, however, that cer-

---

[41] 'Le seul Christ que nous méritons', *avant-propos* to *L'Étranger*, ed. Ray Davison (London: Routledge, 1988), p. vii.

[42] W. B. Yeats, 'The Second Coming'.

[43] See Murray's 'Excursus on the Ritual Form preserved in Greek Tragedy', printed in Jane Ellen Harrison, *Themis: A Study of the Social Origins of Greek Religion* (Cambridge: Cambridge University Press, 1912), pp. 341–63.

[44] *Dithyramb, Tragedy and Comedy* (Oxford: Clarendon Press, 1927), pp. 186–7. For a guarded defence of Nietzsche's contribution to Classical studies see Hugh Lloyd Jones, 'Nietzsche and the Study of the Ancient World', in J. C. O. Flaherty *et al.* (ed.), *Studies in Nietzsche and the Classical Tradition* (Chapel Hill: University of North Carolina Press, 1976), pp. 1–5. Rainer Friedrich, meanwhile, describes Nietzsche's theory of the ritual behind

tain features of Murray's postulated ritual were performed ceremonially at different points in the year. But there is in fact no sign of any unified ritual. As for the phrase *Eniautos Daimon*, we can go a little further. It is not just that it occurs nowhere in the source-material; it could not occur, because it is not possible Greek.

I am saying that it is not only when we assume likeness to ourselves that we distort the past. The very assertion of unlikeness—*especially a weirdly symmetrical unlikeness*—can prove, at a deeper level, to be more in accord with our wishes than with external fact. The twentieth century has been marked by a kind of inverse Narcissism—or by the confounding of the parallel Ovidian myths of Narcissus and the Cyclops (*Metamorphoses*, iii. 341–519; xiii. 840–2). Gazing into the pool of history, it sees, or chooses to see, not the fair face of civil humanity but the shaggy features of the Satyr.

It may be thought that even if this essay has cast doubt on the detailed historical argument of *The Genealogy of Morals*, the effect in the long run is not to subvert but rather to confirm Nietzsche's major thesis, which is precisely a denial of objectivity. That has certainly not been my intention. I have sought to direct the reader not to some great, pulsating, Schopenhauerian negation, but rather to the difficulties of ordinary, piecemeal ignorance. Spectacular cultural subjectivism could never be detected had we no access at all to an object. Not for us, indeed, the unshadowed panoramic clarity of Leonardo's sun-centred Eye. Nor are we offered the converse intoxication of a radical nihilism. We blunder, then correct; we deceive ourselves, but sometimes detect the imposture. It may sound a lot less exciting than the metaphysical extremes, but I firmly believe that, in the long run, it is much more interesting.

Greek tragedy as 'dismal', 'Euripidaristophanizein and Nietzchesokratizein: Aristophanes, Nietzsche and the Death of "Tragedy"', *Dionysius*, vol. iv (1980), pp. 5–36, esp. p. 34.

Freud hedged his bets. As we saw, with half his mind he went for controlling form, but with the other half—I think we may say, with the excited half—he went for real poetic force linked to a potentially destructive libidinal drive. I still feel, however, that the second Freudian scheme is less than persuasive. Contrary to popular belief, the Freudian Death Instinct is not primarily a wish for one's own death but a desire to inflict death on others.[45] Here the rough beast, Apollo's enemy, is given its head. But when we watch a tragedy it seems clear, first, that we identify with the protagonist and, second, that the pleasure of the tragedy is inextricably bound up with a consequent pity, rather than simple exultation over a fallen victim. This fact of identification with the protagonist seems to belong more with the central energy-charge of the drama than with the mitigating formal aspect. The Freudian may say that the pity is itself a disguise-mechanism, to render the pleasure (born in an original, hidden cruelty) morally acceptable to the conscious subject, but at this point in the discussion the ordinary playgoer may begin to rebel. How do we know that the psychoanalyst is not simply constructing in the conveniently un-inspectable area of the Unconscious a solution which is a mere serviceable fiction, its form dictated not by available evidence but simply by the structure of the original problem? 'Pleasure in tragedy looks like cruelty? Why, then, we are cruel, but unconsciously so.' Meanwhile, those who attend to the *oikeia hedone*, 'the proper pleasure', that strange sweetness of grief and fear, will wish to look further.

Nietzsche, somewhat differently from Freud, suggested that tragic pleasure might spring from our sense of re-immersion in pre-individuated consciousness—in the orgiastic unity of the multitude—as the hero dies. This idea has the merit of being founded on a close and intelligent engagement with the actual poetic impact of Greek tragedy. It is

[45] See e.g., *Civilization and its Discontents*, trans. Joan Rivière (London: Hogarth Press, 1963), esp. p. 59.

strikingly true, for example, that the choruses of Greek tragedy, with their Doric dialect, their orgiastic, heavily syncopated rhythms, exist in a kind of tension with the very different verse uttered by the individual persons of the play. But Nietzsche also says that the dying protagonist is always a form of Dionysus himself *and* that Dionysus represents the principle of *anti-*individuation. Surely, on Nietzsche's theory, we cannot rejoice at the demise of *anti-*individuation. *Nietzsche ought to have argued that tragedy dramatized the death of Apollo.*[46] There is in fact no evidence for either thesis, of course.

Once more, one suspects that the *Zeitgeist* is dictating the terms. Nietzsche, like a dozen other anguished, over-introspective post-Romantics, feels a nostalgia for a supposed primal unity. But Greek tragedy, I would venture to suggest, was itself actually pressing in the opposite direction —becoming more and more absorbed by the isolated self standing apart, in contradistinction to the Group. We are driven back to our original problem; back to Aristotle.

I suspect that one thing which makes the Nietzschean and Freudian accounts of the pleasure of tragedy persistently interesting—and I say this in spite of the recent surge of formalism in literary studies—is that they offer a solution rooted not in form but in underlying substance, in human nature. The Aristotelian account, on the other hand, seemed to place its main emphasis on form, and on the palpable unreality of tragedy. Is there a way of reconstruing—or reconstructing—Aristotle's theory in such a way as to give some weight to human substance? I would suggest that for *catharsis*, 'purgation', we substitute 'exercise'. *Catharsis* implies a passive experience, a mere loss of dangerous emotion; 'exercise' implies an active use of emotion. 'Use of emotion' is more than a little reminiscent of Martha Nussbaum's interpretation of the *Poetics*. I wish Aristotle had

[46] Note that this formula is much closer to the sequence in Euripides' *Bacchae*.

not chosen 'purgation', but that, I fear, is what he did. It has been suggested that in frightening dreams the subject can as it were experience disaster without actually experiencing it (I am exploiting an old ambiguity in the term 'experience'). In this way, perhaps, we are able to practise for crises.[47] When the real emergency arrives, it is not, so to speak, our first time. I do not know whether this general theory is true, but I do want to suggest that something of the sort may happen with tragedy. For the process to work, two things need to be the case: first, the situation must be hypothetical rather than categorical (as football is hypothetical warfare, not actual) and, second, that it should nevertheless involve a probable relation to real danger; if there is no probability to face, the exercise will not be testing, will not energize. The simultaneous presence of hypothesis and probable mimesis means that our theory is still Aristotelian, but I have now substituted an active term for the passive *catharsis*. The human capacity to think provisionally, to do thought-experiments, to form hypotheses, to imagine what may happen before it happens—is fundamental to our nature and to our spectacular biological success (so far). I think the cleverest thing Sir Karl Popper ever said was his remark that our hypotheses 'die in our stead'.[48] The human race has found a way, if not to abolish, then to defer and

[47] For the shift within psychoanalysis from the Freudian wish-fulfilment model to the 'prospective' model as associated with Jung and also with Adler's notion of dream as 'dress-rehearsal', see Norman MacKenzie, *Dreams and Dreaming* (London: Aldus Books, 1965), pp. 181, 194, 196. Anthony Storr has pointed out in a letter to me (10 June 1992) that Freud wrote of unpleasant dreams, 'These dreams are endeavouring to master the stimulus retrospectively by developing neurosis', *Beyond the Pleasure Principle*, iv, in *The Standard Edition of the Complete Psychological Works of Sigmund Freud*, 24 vols. (London: Hogarth Press), vol. xviii (1955), p. 32. Storr continues, 'For Freud, however, everything is always a manifestation of the past. Why he didn't think of phantasy as rehearsal, as an attempt to master anxieties prospectively, I can't say: but I think it distorts his whole attitude to creativity and man's inventiveness.'

[48] See his essay 'Of Clouds and Clocks', in his *Objective Knowledge: An Evolutionary Approach* (Oxford: Clarendon Press, 1979), pp. 206–55, at p. 244.

diminish the Darwinian treadmill of death. We send our hypotheses ahead, an expendable army, and watch them fall. It is easy to see how the human imagination might begin to exhibit a need, in art, for a death-game, a game in which the muscles of psychic response, fear and pity, are exercised and made ready, through a facing of the worst, which is not yet the real worst.

> The worst is not so long as we can say 'This is the worst'.
>
> (*King Lear*, IV. i. 29)

When hypothesis lapses into actuality one has indeed a corruption of tragedy, and the element of self-trial is replaced by simple cruelty. There is a horrible poem by Martial, about Prometheus chained to his rock (as he is at the beginning of the Greek tragedy). The poem explains how a criminal called Laureolus was actually crucified, in a parallel dramatic presentation:

> Non falsa pendens in cru'ce Laureolus . . .[49]
> On no pretended cross he hung . . .

The mythological dramas of the Roman arena abolished the space between hypothetical and actual suffering: Ixion on a real burning wheel, one playing the part of Mucius Scaevola burning his hand off in a brazier, the shirt of Nessus by which Hercules meets his agonizing death in Sophocles' *Trachiniae*—'the intolerable shirt of flame'—realized in the unspeakable *tunica molesta* of the circus.[50] A snuff tragedy is not a tragedy.

But what about our own horror videos? This, I confess, I find difficult. Setting aside those alleged cases in which actual death or mutilation is exhibited (these, I take it,

---

[49] *De Spectaculis*, vii, in *Martial: Epigrams*, with an English translation by Walter C. A. Ker, 2 vols. (London: Heinemann, 1947), vol. i, p. 6.

[50] Martial, *Epigrams*, X. xxv. 5, in Ker's edn., ii. 172. Compare Juvenal, *Satires*, VIII. 235. See also John Pearson, *Arena: The Story of the Colosseum* (London: Thames and Hudson, 1973), pp. 96–7 and Roland Auguet, *Cruelty and Civilisation: The Roman Games* (London: George Allen and Unwin, 1971), pp. 100–2.

would be directly analogous to performances in the Roman arena), we are left with a very large number of people enjoying the spectacle of stimulated horror. I do not believe that this pleasure need be sadistic, any more than the tragic pleasure need be so. Indeed I strongly suspect that my notion of energies quickened by a kind of psychic exercise applies here also, but in an arrested form; I suspect, that is, that in the horror video (on which I am no expert) the hypothetical experience is not carried through to its fully human conclusion, in pity and fear. The notion of a facing of the worst, the cognitive element, is only half-present.

In his poem 'Lapis Lazuli' Yeats baited the moralizing figures of his day with the pleasure of tragedy. 'Hamlet and Lear are gay', he wrote, deliberately choosing the most irresponsible word (though little suspecting the meaning it would carry in the late twentieth century). And in 'An Irish Airman Foresees his Death'—also against the grain of high moral sentiment—Yeats had written:

> Nor law nor duty bade me fight,
> Nor public men, nor cheering crowds,
> A lonely impulse of delight
> Drove to this tumult in the clouds.

It is an attitude sometimes described as aesthetic but, notice, it does not circumscribe art, in separation from life. Rather, it links art to a very serious, incorrigibly pleasurable game of death.

Many games are exciting. Tragedy differs from most games in that it requires a peculiar stillness in the watcher together with strenuous activity in that watcher's sympathetic imagination. Above all, it leads to a *conclusion* (which the airman, as long as he is 'dicing with death', must avoid). Of all the literary genres tragedy is the one which lays the heaviest emphasis on ending, and the ending is a mimesis of a death. In so far as we sympathize, we experience the dying, but of course we do not die. The hypothesis dies instead.

We should remember that Aristotle's *catharsis*, a term we have rejected, was coined in part to account for the difference between the behaviour of a sporting crowd and that of a theatre audience. But perhaps the notion of an accomplished conclusion will help here also. Football matches end only because an allotted time runs out. There is no internally necessary terminus. Therefore the excited spectator may well come away with a sense of unfinished business.

I have argued for a basis in human nature for tragic pleasure, but of course form has its part to play. It may be that the special impact of tragedy lies in fact in an eerie coincidence of depicted story and psychic effect. I have said that the spectator achieves a moment of recognition, faces a truth known to be necessary for all. Meanwhile, within the fiction the protagonist is commonly brought to a point of crucial recognition and insight. Sophoclean tragedy is like this. Shakespeare, on the other hand, might prove troublesome.

4

KING LEAR

To move in one stride from Sophocles to Shakespeare may seem, to certain persons, historically licentious, or else merely silly. The not-so-covert presumption of this book, that tragedy is somehow One Thing, is at last exposed for the absurdity it is; in fact there are Greek tragedies, Roman tragedies, Elizabethan, Jacobean, neo-classical; each of these kinds is distinct; Aristotle was talking about one of them and one only; there is no reason to suppose that his remarks will be applicable in any way to the others.

Certainly the fact that they are all called 'tragedies' does not mean that they must share a common essence. Wittgenstein memorably attacked this notion when he challenged the reader to produce an element common to all *games*:[1] in fact, he suggested, the word 'game' connotes a sort of family tree, one game linked to the next by one element, another by another, and so on. The case of tragedy, it might be urged, is similar. Greek tragedy, according to this account, may now be seen as great-aunt, say to Elizabethan tragedy (and how much have *you* in common with your great-aunt?).

I agree of course that Greek tragedy is not the same as Elizabethan. But we misuse our intelligence if we *always* look for difference and never for similarity. We may sneer, for example, at the person who thinks *arrogant* and *proud* have the same meaning, but these words meanwhile clearly *overlap* in meaning and anyone who cannot see the overlap is merely foolish in another way. If we apply the searchlight

---
[1] *Philosophical Investigations*, 66–7, trans. G. E. M. Anscombe (Oxford: Basil Blackwell, 2nd edn., 1958), pp. 31–2.

of differentiation we shall rapidly discover not only that
Elizabethan tragedy differs from Greek, but that Shakespearean tragedy differs from Marlovian, that *King Lear* is
utterly distinct from *Othello*, that the Quarto and Folio
texts of *King Lear* actually furnish the readers with two
plays, not one. The terminus of such analysis is always a
universe of windowless, monadic individuals, linguistically
unassimilable, in which, as Bishop Butler put it, 'Everything
is what it is, and not another thing'.[2] These are occasions
when the Bishop's words are very useful, but they must
not be allowed uncontested sway. Every person we meet is
unique, but they are all people. The word 'people' in the
last sentence is not a piece of grotesque stereotyping. In like
manner plays by Sophocles, Shakespeare, and Racine can
all be tragedies. Wittgenstein would allow this at once but
would add, 'Nevertheless there is no common element,
merely a network of connections.' At this point we need to
move more carefully. For, if the suggestion is that the works
known to us as tragedies are no more unified than are the
Campbells or the Kennedys, then I must resist. The element
of the great person destroyed is not universal in tragedy but
it is insistently repeated, over and over again. A sad ending
is not essential for Greek tragedy but it became so for later
tragedy—and by far the greater number of *Greek* tragedies
involve the destruction of the protagonist. The area of 'overlap' is in fact immense. If I am to be pedantic, I will say that
this book is about those tragedies which depict the destruction of great persons (that is, most of them).

I strongly suspect, meanwhile, that people have been
over-persuaded by Wittgenstein's own example, *game*. Is
there really no element or characteristic common to all
games? Every game I can think of is, on its own terms, a
consciously impractical activity, in which we take part not in
order to produce a concrete result but, as we say, for the fun

² Preface to the Sermons, in *The Works of Joseph Butler*, ed. W. E.
Gladstone, 2 vols. (Oxford: Clarendon Press, 1896), vol. ii, p. 25.

of the thing. The fact that Jane may be competing in the tournament to advance her political career is no embarrassment to my case. My point is that her shots on the snooker table directly affect the outcome of the game only; what Jane subsequently does with that outcome may indeed be serious business and no game at all. This is to imply that from the point of view of the urgently practical person all games will appear in some degree frivolous—and they do. The matter is of some moment if we consider Wittgenstein's own use of the term 'game' elsewhere in his later philosophy: the idea of a 'language game' austerely insinuates a sense of irresponsible detachment, a feeling that what had been seen as contradiction, say, will now melt into mere confusion of grammar or of convention. In fact language is not a game but a very serious business. Nor are particular sectors of discourse—legal language, say, or political—areas of sportive freedom within the grim fact of language itself. They too are serious business. It is true, however, that the special structures of poetry, drama, and fiction are not directly linked to this practical world. That is why I have been able to call Tragedy, oxymoronically, a 'game of death'. But I was consciously straining the term when I used it so: the element of frivolity is there, but is cancelled almost before it is perceived.

Traditionally, most of the answers offered to the question, 'Why does tragedy give pleasure?', have been founded on the essential unreality of tragic drama, on our implicit awareness that what we are looking at is a representation, and not the thing itself. Therefore, while the dramatist may be straining, within the mimesis, for an uncompromising despair, that same dramatist will at the same time preserve a scrupulous loyalty to certain satisfying laws of form, which, if they do not compromise the despair, serve in the long run to mitigate it, which is almost the same thing. Ever since Aristotle pointed out that emotions felt in the theatre are hypothetical rather than categorical—that is, that we weep at the thought of what would happen rather than as at an actual disaster—the pleasure of tragedy has been linked to its palpable unreality; for the hypothetical, unlike the categorical, is within our control, and our secure sovereignty is manifested in the stately artistic form we confer upon it.

There is something odd, in this picture. Sophocles' *Oedipus Rex* is praised because of the unflinching presentation of the blinding of the hero, but this gives pleasure because it is unreal. It is as if theoretical approval and audience engagement are somehow running on separate rails. C. S. Lewis brought out the proper discomfort of the position in the course of a review of George Steiner's *The Death of Tragedy*. Steiner had said that the starkest suffering was 'hallowed' in tragedy. Lewis first queried whether this was true of many very famous tragedies and then added,

An even more disquieting question arises in my mind. Is such hallowing a usual, or frequent, result of undeserved and irreparable disaster in the real world? And if it is not, what claim has the art which depicts it to be a specially stark insight into human life? Can we wholly avoid the suspicion that tragedy as Mr Steiner conceives it is our final attempt to see the world as the world is not?[3]

Lewis is pushing the inwardly weak term 'hallowing' away from the mimetic, towards the formal end of the spectrum. The suggestion thus grows that it is by the *imposition* of grandeur on stories of suffering that they are rendered pleasurable. The celebrated magnitude of tragedy—Aristotle's *megethos*—turns out to be as much a modifier as an intensifier of grief—and all because it is either *propagating* a lie, 'Suffering ennobles', or else because it is tacitly *confessing* one, 'Look—it's all right—this obviously isn't a real blinding. It's all much too grand.' It is often assumed that comedy is a lesser form than tragedy, more self-indulgent, less willing to face harsh reality. Lewis's suggestion interestingly

---

[3] 'Tragic Ends', *Encounter*, vol. xviii (Feb. 1962), pp. 97–102, esp. p. 98.

turns the tables on this prejudice, by implying that tragedy may be the more evasive of the two, subliming pain through the low magic of a formal usurpation, glorifying the inglorious.

This, nevertheless, has been since Aristotle's time the dominant explanation: tragedy gives to pitiable and terrible events a palpably fictitious grandeur; by re-casting suffering in a hypothetical form it releases our emotions from immediate practical responsibility and by rendering it majestic permits actual enjoyment. We can, in our inmost hearts, be comfortable, because form is here controlling matter. If we look at the Apollonian precision, the marvellous interlocked inevitability of *Oedipus Rex*, the theory 'feels right'. If we look at Racine, where the most turbulent and depraved desires are held in Alexandrines of icy perfection, the theory, again, feels right. But what about Shakespeare?

I propose at this point to set the problem of the pleasure of tragedy on one side—to leave it ticking like a time bomb at the back of the reader's mind, while I consider Shakespeare's plays, in a circuitous manner.

In 1808 A. W. von Schlegel coined the term 'tragedies of thought' in connection with Shakespeare's earlier work—especially *Hamlet*.[4] Anyone can see that the earlier tragic heroes have a high IQ; they are very conscious, reflective people (in this at once engaging the interest of S. T. Coleridge who was himself almost pathologically reflective). They offer the spectacle of action impeded or endlessly anticipated by thought—not only Hamlet but also Brutus in *Julius Caesar* or the King in *Richard II*. In the later tragic heroes someone like Eysenck would have no difficulty in detecting a drop in IQ—in Othello, Lear, Antony, Coriolanus. Hence Bradley's remark about transposing Hamlet and Othello

[4] See his *A Course of Lectures on Dramatic Art and Literature*, trans. John Black, 2 vols. (London: [no publisher given] 1815), vol. ii, p. 192. See also A. C. Bradley, *Shakespearean Tragedy*, 2nd edn. (London: Macmillan, 1952), p. 82.

into each other's plays:[5] Othello told by a ghost to kill, simply acts at once; Hamlet, meeting Iago, runs rings round him; each play is stopped in its tracks.

I suspect that the artistic problems of the young Shakespeare were a little different from those which beset most young poets. Where others are usually struggling to express themselves, to find the happy phrase or telling image, Shakespeare found that he could do everything instantly, hit every verbal target, clinch every quibble with an ease which was itself mysteriously disabling. This can be seen most clearly in the early comedy *Love's Labours Lost.* This play about the defeat of academic discourse at the hands of sexual love is itself an explosion of joyous verbal ingenuity. The young men, particularly Berowne, crackle with premature articulateness and have to be slowed down by the ladies (could there be a sexual analogy somewhere behind this sentence?). Berowne cannot speak without a delighted, separate awareness of the formal character of his own utterance and this kind of intelligence is, as Rosaline teaches him, the enemy of love (think how, in a later comedy, Beatrice and Benedick have to be delivered by a stratagem of their friends, from wit to love).

> BEROWNE   My love to thee is sound, sans crack or flaw.
> ROSALINE   Sans sans, I pray you.
> BEROWNE   Yet I have a trick
>   Of the old rage; bear with me, I am sick.
>
> (V. ii. 415–17)

At the end of the play Berowne is made to do penance for his articulateness; he is sent to tell his jokes in a hospital, his marriage postponed.

This penance Shakespeare, evidently, is simultaneously imposing on himself. For the proper conclusion of the *play* —the marriage—is denied, with the news of death brought

---

[5] *Shakespearean Tragedy,* p. 142.

by the man in black, with the sudden chill in the air as the lovers draw apart.

> Our wooing doth not end like an old play,
> Jack hath not Jill.
>
> (V. ii. 862–3)

The moral of this most dazzlingly verbal of plays is that words must defer at last to a reality which is other than they. 'Il n'y a pas de hors-texte', writes Derrida.[6] 'Oh yes there is,' answers Shakespeare, 'but I indeed am stuck with nothing but words, glassed in with my own—ugh—verbal brilliance.'

In his early Tragedies Shakespeare chose, I would suggest, to set the dog which had been savaging him upon his heroes. *Richard II* has always posed a problem of political realism. In one way Richard is an evident fantasist, turning everything, including his own imminent fate, into a story.

> For God's sake, let us sit upon the ground
> And tell sad stories of the death of Kings.
>
> (III. ii. 185–6)

Yet in another way, Richard's insight into the real tendency of events is almost clairvoyant. In the deposition scene, which Walter Pater admirably described as an inverted coronation,[7] Richard is the high camp impresario of his own undoing while Bolingbroke, his usurping successor, looks on with some irritation. The climax comes when Richard sends for a glass and, disappointed to see a comparatively youthful, untragic face, dashes the mirror to the ground, saying,

> Mark silent King, the moral of this sport—
> How soon my sorrow hath destroy'd my face.
>
> (V. i. 290–1)

Bolingbroke answers positivistically,

> The shadow of your sorrow hath destroy'd
> The shadow of your face.
>
> (V. i. 292–3)

---

[6] *De La Grammatologie* (Paris: Éditions de Minuit, 1967), p. 227.
[7] *Appreciations* (Gowan's International Library, 1910), p. 198.

Bolingbroke's accent is that of the realist, but there is a sense in which his minimizing reply is merely stupid. Great things *are* being enacted on the stage.

For all that, the sense that Richard is somehow glassed in with words remains strong. It is as if he knows everything about his situation except the fact that it is actually happening to him. Only in the penultimate scene of the drama does he find, as he plays upon the word 'nothing', a substance not invested in conventional role playing and verbal performance.

> Think that I am unking'd by Bolingbroke
> And straight am nothing. But whate'er I be,
> Nor I, nor any man that but man is,
> With nothing shall be pleas'd till he be eas'd
> With being nothing.
>
> (V. v. 31–5)

The cadence of thought needs to be followed with care. Behind the continuing, Ricardian chiming of word with word, there is a crucial slippage, from form to matter, from air to earth. The first 'nothing', in 'straight am nothing', has all the weakness of that unconstrained hyperbole which a universe of discourse so liberally affords. But the last nothing is quite different; it means 'death'. The sentence repents as Berowne had to repent, of its own formalism. Richard implicitly confesses that, though unkinged, though conventionally dismantled, *he is in fact still here*, that there will be a Richard who suffers until Richard actually dies.

Thus the protagonist begins to turn, on the vanishing word 'nothing', from a tissue of words into a human being, at the end of the play. The action of *King Lear* begins with the same word, 'nothing', a huge, ragged hole in the fabric of verbal interchange.

> LEAR   What can you say to draw
>   A third more opulent than your sisters? Speak.
> CORDELIA   Nothing, my lord.

LEAR   Nothing!
CORDELIA Nothing.
LEAR   Nothing will come of nothing. Speak again.

(I. i. 85–90)

Lear is no Richard, for we have left the tragedies of thought. He is unreflective, he 'hath ever but slenderly known himself' (I. i. 293). He is the greatest of all the tragic heroes of the later passional phase. The opening encounter with Cordelia unites, in a peculiarly Shakespearean way, immense dramatic power with extraordinary subtlety. I think I despair of ever explaining it, though in a good performance everyone understands it. We want to say, 'Cordelia answers as she does because she is a truth-teller.' But what is the truthful answer to Lear's question, 'Who loves me best?' It is 'Cordelia'. Yet she, the good daughter, cannot produce either the simplicity or the warmth her father asks for. She with the intensified intelligence of the adolescent, cannot but perceive that she is trapped by the King's question in a mercenary game, carrying a huge material reward, which she must refuse to play. Note that her intelligence is the opposite of Berowne's; he is so intent upon the verbal medium that he cannot look steadily on the reality; she is so aware of the human context that language is curtailed, she cannot heave her heart into her mouth. To express love warmly would in this situation create a presumption of continuity with the flattery offered by her sisters; a wholly honourable *amour-propre* comes into play and inhibits her speech. But think of the difficulty of explaining the term *amour-propre* to Lear. 'I want her to love *me*' would be his answer. Lear, conversely, is so lacking in awareness that he can scarcely perceive the difference between game-playing and serious action. 'Who loves Daddy best?'—'Cordelia!'—gives her a sweet—is, one suspects, the pattern of the back of his mind, which is all right, as long as Cordelia is small enough to climb on his knee. But not now. This I suspect is why, in that half-strangled quantification of love which so eerily anticipates the mathematical love subtraction exercise by her sisters later (II. iv. 247–62), she speaks of the amount of love which must be set aside for her husband (I. i. 98– 103). She is partly striving to convey the message, 'I am not a little girl now, I will be getting married.' She is anxious not to patronize (notice the inversion implied in the etymology of that word) her father; she could, as it were, pat him on the head and give him the hug he asks for, but to do so would be to insult his understanding (though at another level it would not have been wrong).

'So young and so untender?' asks the King. 'So young, my lord, and true', answers Cordelia (I. i. 106–7). That last word, 'true', needs an Empson for its explication. The primary sense must be the ethical one, 'faithful', but obviously the epistemological meaning 'truth-telling', is not absent, but rather is embarrassingly importunate, in the background. It is a priggish answer and a deeply loving one. It is indeed a young person's answer. It infuriates the King.

What has happened in this opening scene? A dance-like composition of fairy-tale simplicity—an old King, three daughters of whom two are wicked and one is good— splinters into extreme psychological realism, and breaks down in an abortion of dialogue. This sequence is then pitilessly re-enacted in the play which follows. The fairy-tale eucatastrophe of the earlier anonymous drama of *Leir* is smashed. Indeed, to borrow Berowne's words, this tragedy doth not end like the old play. Consider the majesty—the moral majesty—which Shakespeare has chosen to destroy.

Lear at the beginning is a wilful, unthinking monarch, an unconscious tyrant of his children's affections. His perception of England as he explains the map at the beginning is a purblind-aristocratic one: good salmon fishing here, good hunting there—'with shadowy forests and with champains rich'd, / With plenteous rivers and wide skirted meads' (I. i. 643). Later this comfortable king is made to see the underside of England, naked wretches, beggars driven from poor farm gates by dogs, the deranged roaring figures described by Edgar, who stick nails in their arms to enforce charity (IV. vi. 158; II. iii. 15). The King, cast into the wilderness by his own daughters, learns even as his wits begin to turn (III. iv. 21) to feel pity and to accept responsibility: 'Oh I have ta'en / Too little care of this' (III. iv. 32–3). In his madness he begins to acquire the moral wisdom of a charity he could not compass when he was sane.

In the Chronicle, when Cordelia returns with the French army, she wins and places her father on the throne. It might be thought that Shakespeare exercised his maximum destructive energy, when he turned this victory into defeat. The truth is a good deal more painful. For Shakespeare continues the music of eucatastrophe, beyond the point of material defeat, thus giving it an inescapably spiritual power —a Christian power. Lear and his daughter, hauled off to prison, are in charity both with each other and with their captors. The emotional tyrant of Act I now wishes to kneel to his own daughter and is luminously benevolent to his very gaolers. It is possible to think at this point of the play, 'Nothing that these people can do to them now can destroy this love, itself formed by an extremity of suffering; because it transcends material humiliation it is full Christian charity, something stronger than pain or death.'

But as we all know, something more can be done to them, and is done. As with *Love's Labours Lost* we found ourselves saying that *Shakespeare* had to mortify his own facility in speech, so here, more grimly, we must say that Shakespeare has not finished with Lear and Cordelia. It is the ending Johnson could not bear, the killing of Cordelia. When Lear enters, howling, with Cordelia dead in his arms, which is he more like, the archaic King of the opening (now carried to a much greater power), or the figure of universal charity we saw at the beginning of V. iii? 'I killed the slave that was a-hanging thee,' he says, to his dead child. A gust of approval passes through the audience. Think for a moment how impossible it would be, how profoundly unacceptable, for Lear to have said, 'I turned my own cheek for a blow to the man I found a-hanging thee': it is as if, by killing Cordelia before the King, Shakespeare has quickened ancient moral energies which Christianity cannot, after all, effortlessly transcend. Suddenly the burning charity of the scene's opening seems a faint thing, when set beside this grief, this rage.

I have described this episode as a terrible, last-minute wrenching, almost a vandalism of the spirit, in which a story of descent and re-ascent, harrowing of hell followed by regeneration and redemption, is wantonly smashed with a degree of pain sufficient to make the earlier exposure to the storm a slight thing by comparison. But Shakespeare's ending is not simply tacked on. Shakespeare is Shakespeare and he has prepared his ground. Even within the speech of luminous charity I have referred to he plants certain signs of a passion still unspent (Nicholas Brooke's phrase).[8]

> So we'll live, and pray, and sing,
> And tell old tales, and laugh
> At gilded butterflies, and hear poor rogues
> Talk of court news; and we'll talk with them too—
> Who loses and who wins; who's in, who's out—
> And take upon's the mystery of things
> As if we were God's spies.
>
> (V. iii. 11–17)

The dominant note is one of transcendent love but it is not the only note struck. Lear instead of attempting to reassert his power offers to become a friendly gossip on the power-relations of others. 'The mystery of things', given this context, must be a pivotal word, in which the sense 'court secrets' is overtaken by the sense 'divine mystery', as it is uttered. The obstinately troubling word is 'spies', a sinister word in Shakespeare's time as in ours. One strains to reclaim

---

[8] *Shakespeare's King Lear* (London: Edward Arnold, 1963), p. 51.

the image for pure charity, by saying that Shakespeare is
thinking simply of viewing, or glimpsing in the distance
(compare *Romeo and Juliet*, IV. i. 68, 'I do spy a kind of
hope'): Lear and Cordelia are now seeing everything differently, as if from some high, sunlit tower. But the darker
meaning, stronger in any case in the noun 'spy' than in the
verb, will not quite go away. Dr Johnson said that the word
referred to 'angels commissioned to survey and report the
lives of men'.[9] That Lear and Cordelia should be rendered
angelic by this line is what the party for pure charity desires,
but the *office* of such angels may be more involved with
punishment than love. The best support I know for Johnson's reading comes from Shakespeare's play about revenge,
Hamlet, from an exchange between Claudius and the tensely
hostile Prince. The King tells Hamlet that he is to go to
England and Hamlet says 'Good'. The King answers, 'Good
it is, if you knew our purposes', and Hamlet replies, '*I see a
cherub that sees them*' (IV. iii. 47–9). Here the implication is
that the cherub's office is to spy out evil. If we carry the
meaning back into the 'God's spies' line in *King Lear*, we
may sense that revenge has not been wholly dissolved in
universal love, but may have been passed on, to an Old
Testament God whose proper work it is.

The precise effect of the word 'spies' will always, I dare
say, be controversial. Indeed it is, I believe, deliberately
unclear in its moral resonance. But no one can deny a
blazing clarity in the lines which follow:

> Upon such sacrifices, my Cordelia,
> The gods themselves throw incense. Have I caught thee?
> He that parts us shall bring a brand from heaven
> And fire us hence like foxes. Wipe thine eyes;
> The good years shall devour them, flesh and fell,
> Ere they shall make us weep. We'll see 'em starved first.
>
> (V. iii. 20–5)

[9] *Johnson on Shakespeare*, ed. Arthur Sherbo, 2 vols., being vols. vii and
viii of the Yale Edition of the Works of Samuel Johnson, 15 vols. (New Haven
and London: Yale University Press, 1958–85), vol. viii (1968), p. 700.

The first two lines smell marvellous sweet and speak of sacrifice, perhaps with reference to renunciation of worldly power. But with the shift to the *plural* 'gods' (I am convinced that 'God' in 'God's spies' is, uniquely in this play, a singular—apostrophe 's', not 's' apostrophe)—with this shift to the plural there is a faint diminution of force. Then come the lines expressing the love of the person *against* the whole world, when tenderness to the child and sheer ferocity towards anyone who would come between them are a single, fully human thing. These lines make the universal love of the theologians look like a sanctimonious fiction. It is as if the Christian doctrine of loving one's enemies can seem magnificent as long as those enemies confine their destructive energies to oneself; when the torturers turn on one's child, is it *still* admirable to love them? I suppose the strongest Christian will say yes, but I am sure that Shakespeare knows that at this point, in the audience, the Old Adam will assert himself, exactly as the old Lear is heard once more in the poetry.

The ethical violence of this is for me echoed in a passage in C. S. Lewis's *A Grief Observed*, the book in which he set down a record of his experience of bereavement, after the death of his wife. This death, this grief was quite clearly a shock to his Christianity, as the earlier death of his friend Charles Williams had not been. Lewis wrote of the earlier experience, 'When the idea of death and the idea of Williams met in my mind, it was the idea of death which was changed.'[10] When his wife died the pain of loss was too great for such transcending thoughts. Instead we are given words which tear a great rent in conventional piety:

Once very near the end I said, 'If you can—if it is allowed—come to me when I too am on my death bed.' 'Allowed', she said. 'Heaven would have a job to hold me, and as for Hell, I'd break it into bits.'[11]

[10] Preface to *Essays Presented to Charles Williams* (London: Oxford University Press, 1947), p. xiv.
[11] *A Grief Observed* (London: Faber, 1966), p. 63.

Dr Johnson saw that Shakespeare had broken a beautiful, given story. He wrote, 'Shakespeare has suffered the virtue of Cordelia to perish in a just cause, contrary to the natural ideas of justice, to the hope of the reader, and, what is yet more strange, to the faith of chronicles.'[12] Kenneth Muir in the New Arden edition sought to weaken the impact of this by observing that in fact 'in all the sources known to have been used by Shakespeare with the one exception of the old play, Cordelia commits suicide'.[13] The comment is designed to make Johnson look slightly foolish, imperfectly informed. It is true that in Spenser's version, in Holinshed, and in John Higgins's poem in *The Mirror for Magistrates*, Cordelia does indeed die by her own hand. But what Muir ought in justice to have explained is that in all three *the Lear story* ends with Lear and Cordelia together, the King restored to his kingdom. Thereafter the King dies a natural death and is succeeded by Cordelia. The suicide of Cordelia is the result of a later sequence of events in which her nephews rise against her. Johnson's sentence is perfectly correct. Shakespeare goes flat against the Chronicles.

Johnson complained that Shakespeare failed to observe poetic justice in *King Lear*—that is, he failed to ensure that the good end happily. This is an odd complaint, to say the least, because it is characteristic of tragedy that it should affront poetic justice. The suffering of the protagonist must be terrible, not merely fair. *Macbeth*, it is often said, is in danger of slipping from the tragic because its hero is so wicked, with the consequence that the conclusion is *too* 'poetically just'—the dead butcher brought down—and so perhaps a matter as much for satisfaction as for pity or terror. But one suspects that Johnson was stung to his oddly inapposite complaint by the fact that the story of Lear, in its central inherited form, is a kind of Christian *commedia* in

---

[12] *Johnson on Shakespeare*, vol. viii, p. 704.
[13] *King Lear*, the new Arden edition by Kenneth Muir (London: Methuen, 1959), p. xxxiv.

which the good win through to felicity. He rightly senses violation. Other strong Christians, such as Tolstoy, had similar feelings.

In the 1623 Folio text, but not in the 1608 Quarto, Lear dies with the words, 'Look on her lips, look there, look there.' Apparently he sees some movement in the feather laid on Cordelia's face and thinks that she is alive. He dies, shaken with an excess of joy. A. C. Bradley, driven, one suspects, by the same unreadiness to endure this text which Johnson experienced so many years before, came close to arguing that Lear in his last words was admitted to a vision of life beyond death. The suggestion is faint but somehow intensely proffered. Bradley understands perfectly that Lear dies mistaken, but he says that Cordelia is something 'calm and bright and still', a being independent of the dreadful events of the drama, and that she is 'rather set free from life than deprived of it'.[14] These thoughts correspond to Lewis's thoughts of Charles Williams. When the idea of death and the idea of Cordelia met in Bradley's mind it was the idea of death that was changed, but in truth it is the pain of the later passage, in *A Grief Observed*, that is closer to Shakespeare's play.

In 1623 (not 1608), Lear dies in a state of joy, but this seems only to deepen pathos, and the pathetic is not the same thing as the tragic. In fact, by a further stroke of cruelty, Shakespeare at the end of the play withholds tragic *anagnorisis*—ultimate recognition—from his hero. *Anagnorisis* in Aristotle is normally a simple recognition of some long-lost loved person, as it might be through signs or tokens. But in a couple of places (*Poetics*, 1452 a 33, 1455 a 17) he says the best recognition is the one in Sophocles' *Oedipus Rex*, where the recognition arises not from tokens but from incidents. In *Oedipus Rex* the protagonist learns *his own* identity, and this clarifies and gives dignity to his

---

[14] *Shakespearean Tragedy*, pp. 317, 324.

downfall. Because of the central, Oedipal example the term *anagnorisis* can easily take on the more general meaning 'recognition of the underlying truth'. This generalized notion has had a long and fruitful critical history. Some theorists such as Dorothea Krook regard final insight as 'a universal element of tragedy'.[15] Now in *King Lear* this does not happen. Instead, a deeply moving moral anagnorisis is set up in the middle-to-later part of the play and then erased at the end. If the Folio text is, as the Oxford editors suggest,[16] a revision made two or three years after the first version of the play has been written and performed, we may suppose that Shakespeare was not content with the mere absence of final insight. In the Quarto, Lear says, 'Pray you undo / This button. Thank you sir. O, O, O, O!', Edgar says, 'He faints', and then, to Lear, 'My lord, my lord!', and Lear speaks in answer not to Edgar but to his own pain, 'Break heart, I prithee, break.' These are his last words. In the Quarto, Lear, indeed, is given no final understanding but he is given, so to speak, a king's privilege: he issues a command which is obeyed. There is the faintest of analogies with Oedipus in this assumption of command; he wills his own destruction. But in the Folio revision Lear is given what seems to be a moment of perception, a sudden intuition (of life in the dead child)—but an intuition which is wholly mistaken. The full splendour of *anagnorisis* is present for a moment but present only, it would seem, to be denied. By actually providing a false *anagnorisis* at the end Shakespeare makes his rejection of the final, classical insight completely inescapable.

I do not, then, conclude that the idea of protagonistic *anagnorisis* is irrelevant to this play. Rather I think that Shakespeare wrote with a sense that something of the sort

[15] *Elements of Tragedy* (New Haven and London: Yale University Press, 1969), p. 8.
[16] William Shakespeare, *The Complete Works*, general editors Stanley Wells and Gary Taylor (Oxford: Clarendon Press, 1988), p. 943.

was expected, so that its cancellation would be *felt*—in an inarticulate way, no doubt—as a withholding or denial rather than as an inert absence. He did a similar thing at the end of *Othello* where the hero is given a big speech having all the formal marks of ultimate *anagnorisis* but notably lacking the thing itself—Othello's last words proudly record a state of extreme perplexity. Lear dies not knowing and this is a stroke against *tragedy itself*.

It is of course an editorial accident which produced the inco-ordinate division of Shakespeare's plays into Comedies, Histories, and Tragedies. *Richard II*, telling the story of the death of a king, is a more perfect tragedy than the almost bourgeois *Othello*. And *Richard II* terminates, satisfyingly, in *anagnorisis*. But *King Lear* moves from the initial rupture of the word 'nothing' to a more comprehensive rejection of the end—an uncomprehending death.

It is perhaps no accident (as sloppy-minded people say when they cannot work out the precise connection) that this play contains the most extraordinary moment of audience disorientation in all drama. It is as if Shakespeare wished to extend the inner principle of nescience to the spectators. I mean the moment known irrationally as 'Dover Cliff'—irrationally because, as it turns out, Dover Cliff was not its setting. Edgar, as mad Tom, induces the newly blinded Gloucester to believe that he is ascending a steep hill, near the sea (IV. vi. 1–6). He then explains that they are on a dizzy height, with the waves breaking far below them. Gloucester asks Edgar to withdraw some paces and then hurls himself, as he supposes, from the cliff edge. He falls prone, on level ground. Edgar draws near again, now pretending to be a countryman, and exclaims in wonder that Gloucester can be alive after such a fall.

It is a sequence having some of the characteristics of farce—banana skin jokes, the lunatic leading the blind and so on. But there is seldom any trouble with unwanted audience laughter. No doubt this is partly because of the sheer human horror involved, the blindness and the grief (but horror, notice, does not stop audiences laughing at Webster). I suspect the presence of a further, technical reason. A man slipping on a banana skin can be funny to one watching *ab extra*; it is not so for the person slipping. Edgar's description of the terrible drop from the cliff edge involves the audience in Gloucester's error, often, I suspect, to the point of complete, if temporary, delusion. Jacobean audiences, accustomed to rudimentary scenery, were educated to trust verbal indications of place—'Here on this wild moor' and the like. I can remember the first time I saw *King Lear* as a child and I am pretty sure that I thought for a moment or two that Gloucester had fallen from a cliff—and then corrected myself. It is a difficult point to make with sophisticated students of Shakespeare, because they tend to be too clearly aware of what is happening in the scene. But even with such an audience the vertigo speech is so strong that it engages a temporary excess of imaginative assent, after which Gloucester's fall can never have the kind of objectivity required by farce. There is moreover a sign that Shakespeare may have succeeded in confusing *himself,* for much later in the scene Edgar says, 'Here in the sands thee I'll rake up' (IV, vi. 275), as if they really were on a beach (it is *just* possible, I suppose, that he is reverting to the pretence for his father's benefit). The episode remains unique. We are thrown, like Gloucester, into darkness, though his darkness, unlike ours, is continued.

What, then, can be the pleasure of *this* tragedy? I suggested at the beginning of this chapter that tragedy was able to please because it showed the worst we can imagine ennobled by form, disposed in a stately progression, with that kind of intelligible sequence which is ultimately eloquent of control. But in *King Lear* destruction is not halted at the level of the protagonist; it extends itself to the *form* of his descent and engulfs the spectator. The dramatist is, we begin to feel, strangely cruel. The eeriest moment in the play is when Edgar tells Gloucester that, before he fell, there was a devil close at the blind man's ear (exactly where he, Edgar, had been standing a moment before). When Christ went out into the wilderness the devil came to him and urged him to cast himself down from a pinnacle (Matthew 4: 6; Luke 4: 9). It will be said that Edgar is teaching Gloucester that the impulse to commit suicide is diabolical and that he should trust in the divine power which has miraculously preserved his life after so great a fall. But we have by this time become aware that there was no miracle, that Edgar has played upon his father's aged condition with highly theatrical mendacity—has lied. This allows, amid the general imaginative disorientation, a queer feeling that Edgar (who, as many have said, seems at times strangely taken over by the mad Tom persona) was for a moment almost devilish in his practising upon the blind man. Because the practice was itself such pure theatre—illusionism—the dramatist is now touched by the same imputation. In the history of the temptation in the wilderness, Christ who is also Creator is tormented by the devil with his own omnipotence—he can fall and save himself. Shakespeare has a power in his plays which could conceivably shake Shakespeare. He pulls the strings that work the puppets. He was standing behind the blind and tortured old man at the edge of that non-existent cliff. I conceded earlier in this chapter that my phrase 'game of death' necessarily implies a grotesque twinge of frivolity, swallowed immediately by the consequence. Shakespeare seems in his own astonishing way to make a parallel concession, in the farcical elements of the 'Dover Cliff' scene: '*Of course* this is all mere, appalling, irresponsible theatre', they seem to say, in a kind of agony. But if Shakespeare is Edgar he is also Gloucester.

It may be that there is a short answer to my question, namely that this is a great work but it does not please; it hurts too much. Neither Tolstoy nor Johnson was a literary idiot. Both in a way hated the play; it is as if the best of us came forward and said 'No' to it. Johnson wrote, 'I was many years ago so shocked by Cordelia's death, that I know not whether I ever endured to read again the last scenes of the play till I undertook to revise them as an editor.'[17] If I may be permitted an old-fashioned ethical term, this seems to me a wholly *honourable* response. I respect it more than I respect much facile praise which has been set down since the time of Johnson.

Yet I do not agree with him. I re-read *King Lear* and, although it shakes me, I enjoy the process. It must be giving me this thing which sounds so puny after the blinding of Gloucester, the death of the bewildered old King—*pleasure*. I have fallen into the use of the first person because it is clear that *King Lear* produces very diverse responses. But it *can* please and I'm not sure that such pleasure is wholly discreditable (though when I read Johnson I was almost ashamed of it). First, in line with the traditional formal theory, Shakespeare, though he worked against grandeur of sequence and structure, does supply *megethos*—magnitude. I once heard a very clever paper by John Carey in which he argued that critics were logically confused in an elementary way: that Lear in his madness was given a crazy magniloquence—manifestly insane hyperbole—and the critics ineptly transpose this magnitude to the play, and prose on about cosmic, universal grandeur and the like. The real voice of the play, said Carey, is quiet, like Cordelia's. Although I have spent so much time arguing that *King Lear* breaks down grand systems, I still want to say obstinately that the critics talk in this way because that is how poetry works. If a play contains a character who speaks vividly and at length about apples, that play will have 'an Autumnal feel', even if the character is not 'commended' by the dramatist. The gigantic utterance of the mad Lear really does give hugeness to the drama. Compare the way Shakespeare chose

---

[17] *Johnson on Shakespeare*, vol. viii, p. 704.

in *Antony and Cleopatra* ethically to humiliate the hero and heroine, but ensured that they would figure as colossi in our imagination by the splendour of poetic utterance given to each. Therefore the most primitive formal requirement in Aristotle, 'bigness', is satisfied.

Aristotle also said, however (*Poetics*, 1448 b 13), that at the very root of mimesis lies a pleasure in learning that this marble is an Athene. This primitive interpretative pleasure may then be replicated in secondary acts of apprehension such as, 'And Athene must indeed be tall and grave of face, like this stone'—leading toward a pleasure in probability or (grander word) truth. There can be little doubt that writers who choose not to enforce but to disrupt grand formal sequences often do so, not with radically deconstructive metaphysical intent, but with at least a presumption that, now, it is the truth that is essayed, rather than some comfortable pattern. And the mind is pleased by *this*, because it is receiving, or thinks it is receiving, real nourishment. Even in time of war one can prefer true bad news to manifestly false good news. For me there is pleasure, therefore, in the play's very refusal to pretend that the good end happily— and this pleasure is the opposite of the formal opiate we spoke of earlier. It may be said that if truth were the seat of literary power, 'London is the largest city in England' would be high poetry. Clearly the kind of truth we are dealing with must be an *embodied* truth, a matter of *connaître* rather than *savoir*, *Erleben* rather than *Wissen*. And, as Aristotle insisted, it will be hypothetical. Poetry can body forth the probable and possible, and this we can properly enjoy. In Sophocles the learning of the audience is conclusively and majestically enforced by its echo in the *anagnorisis* of the protagonist. Aristotle describing the elementary learning pleasure of tragedy says, 'The Reason why we are pleased when we look at pictures is that, as we look, we find ourselves learning and reasoning out what each element is, for example that this, here, is that man' (1448 b 15–17).

The last, oddly colourless phrase (*hoti houtos ekeinos* in the Greek) becomes powerful if we think of Oedipus. His 'recognition of a long-lost person' was the recognition of himself: 'This man, here, is that person to whom Jocasta gave birth; that child is I and I am he.' Shakespeare offers no such clinching, final insight. Instead he teaches a harder lesson: that sufferers may die without knowing why they have suffered. I have suggested that Sophoclean tragedy may indeed owe its special power to a peculiar echoic property, the learning of the protagonist answering to the spectator's encounter with the image of his or her own death. Shakespeare has violently cancelled this formal echo, after certain features of the play had begun to promise it more powerfully than ever before. I have traced this principally in the story of Lear, but it can be seen also in the story of Gloucester. In *Oedipus Rex* blindness is made to enforce by paradox the accession of knowledge: Teiresias, the seer who knows all from the beginning, is also blind from the beginning of the play. Oedipus, when his knowledge at last grows to the point at which it matches that of Apollo, the Solar Eye in heaven, destroys the frail organ of physical sight in himself. The terror serves not to humiliate the protagonist as knower, but to exalt him. Gloucester in *King Lear* is blinded and subjected to a process of spiritual initiation clouded by an element of parodic theatre—by deception and illusion—in which nescience is extended to the audience. But by this means the most fundamental element of all, the audience's sense of having faced the worst, is perhaps strengthened. Nescience, after all, serves a knowledge that is both greater and more modest than the usual cosmic insight of the protagonist, the knowledge that we do not know, that we cannot understand.

It will be seen that I have moved away from a formalist account of the pleasure of tragedy just as I moved away earlier from a Freudian–Nietzschean account of tragedy as a form rooted in black, irrational desires. The direction of my thought, it might be said, is towards an intellectualist theory: tragedy as an exercise in understanding in advance the real horrors we may meet and the psychic violence they may cause. But as I write these words I remember what Craig Raine said to me when I asked him, 'Why does tragedy give pleasure?' 'All emotion is pleasurable', he replied. I think also of words in a letter Anthony Storr wrote to me about the pleasure of tragedy: 'I immediately and prematurely think that *arousal*, in the physiological sense, is itself pleasurable, however dreadful the stimulus. Our craving for excitement of any kind leads to a certain pleasure in reading about a new atrocity or earthquake. We can't bear monotony—see all the stuff about sensory deprivation.' There is in both these responses a combination of simplicity with shrewdness which hits hard. I have laboured long to explain how terror might be pleasurable, as if there were a great mystery here. But at the level of initial arousal even terror is fun, as everyone who has been on a fairground ride knows perfectly well. Can we not, in the face of this obvious truth, cut short our grand theorizing and say simply, 'Pity and fear are fun'?

In fact we cannot. Aristotle's interest was engaged not by the initial thrill experienced by the audience as they sat in the theatre but by their state of mind when the play was over, after the lucid demonstration of a probable or necessary sequence of events leading to the dreadful death of the protagonist. Tragedy, unlike fairground rides, operates not only at the level of arousal but also at the level of conclusion or closure. It is the special pleasure—the *oikeia hedone*—that we feel when all is done, when we have followed the sequence to its terrible end and understood, that still needs to be explained. In giving this answer I do not wish to set aside as irrelevant the pleasure of arousal. There is no doubt that tragedy makes use of this phenomenon. But in tragedy the irresponsible pleasure of arousal is joined with bonds of iron to the responsibilities of probable knowledge and intellectual assent.

We are returned to the theory I offered in my third chapter. In *King Lear* the game of death is played very hard—even to the point of making us aware that all the stately signals of formality are frail, that the rules of language and hypothesis, which make it, still, a game and not death itself, are only temporary defences. When the game is played so hard it is perhaps inevitable that some (and I have said that these are not the worst of us) should actually get hurt.

I will end by saying that, although I have stressed the word 'nothing' and the destruction of authoritative sequences, I do not believe that the play is morally nihilist. The words 'good' and 'evil' mean not less but more to one who has just watched *King Lear*. Nor, by the way, do I regard the problem of tragedy as wholly solved.

Index